The Filthy Five

Bruce F. Katz

Also from Bruce F. Katz

Fiction

The Family Jewels

The History Lesson (a Novel for Young Adults)

Non-Fiction

When Your Name is On the Door

Prologue

August 2016

The detective put down his newspaper, took a deep breath, and exhaled. He'd put the entire 1992 incident so far back in the filing cabinet of his mind he'd completely forgotten it until he picked up this morning's edition of *The Harrisburg Patriot-News*.

It had to happen, of course, he thought. *It was always a question of when, not if.* He stood, took a long look around the squad room, and walked out the door. First, he descended to the basement to retrieve a box containing several thick, well-worn files. Then he climbed two flights of stairs and strode to a door with a frosted glass window marked *CAPTAIN*. He knocked and let himself in.

"Cap?" he asked. "Got a minute?" He placed the file box on an adjacent table.

His boss looked up from a stack of papers.

"A minute is all I have," he said. "Come on in."

"Did you see this in the morning paper?" He tossed it on the captain's cluttered desk. The captain read the brief piece and looked up.

"I wasn't on the force yet when this happened," he said. "But everyone's at least heard about the Garrett Bensen case." He paused. "Do you have something you want to say?"

"Yeah," the detective said, sitting. "Yeah, I do. But it's going to take more than a minute."

He'd never told a soul what he witnessed in that alley that night, twenty-five years earlier. Things were different now. The Harrisburg Police Bureau was different. He was different. He needed to finally report, for the record, what he'd seen back then with his own two eyes.

• • •

"I watched events unfold from a safe place, behind a row of six garbage cans. There were a dozen black vinyl trash bags piled on top and alongside."

The captain settled back in his chair as the detective settled back into memory.

"I was fifteen years old and couldn't process what was happening. I knew I wasn't supposed to be out late that night, and I shouldn't have been downtown. Thankfully, nobody had seen me. I was going to stay put until I could get away unnoticed.

"It was hard for me to hide. As my grandmother

always told me, I may have been big, but I was still growing. I was already over six feet tall and over two hundred pounds. From the back, until you saw my face, I could have been mistaken for a full-grown man.

"I was a good kid. I got good grades and impressed the coaches on defense for the Harrisburg High football team. If it had come down to it, I could have put up a decent fight with any one of those three guys on the ground. The other guy, though—the one who put them on the ground in a matter of seconds—he was another story altogether. He was smaller than all three of the other guys, but it was them on the ground, not him. I watched him deal with each of them, one at a time. But I'm getting ahead of myself.

"I was too far away to see everything that was happening or to hear what anyone was saying. When they first walked into the alley, the three guys were in charge. It looked to me like they were going to bring a whole load of hurt down on the smaller guy. He looked drunk, or something else. One of the three took out a gun—that was when I slipped out of sight behind the trashcans. Another, the big one who looked like he was in charge, told the guy to put the gun away. I heard him say he wanted to use his hands. That didn't work out for him or the others.

"Soon as the guy put the gun away, it was like a switch flipped. Suddenly, this guy—the smaller one— he wasn't drunk anymore. He used *his* hands, *his* feet, and *his* forearms to bring the three of them, first to their knees and then to the ground. I swear, Cap, it only took seconds. But he wasn't done. Not yet."

The detective nodded his head, remembering. He gazed out the window behind the captain's desk, watching the traffic move down Walnut Street toward the bridge crossing the Susquehanna River.

"He moved from one to the next one. He got into each one's face and talked quietly, one on one. I tried to hear but the guy was whispering. I couldn't make it out. There was some conversation. One of them dropped an *n*-bomb. I couldn't figure that out since I was the only Black person in the alley.

"Then the smaller guy . . . he . . . he just killed them. He did it with his bare hands. The first one and the third one, he did quickly. He snapped the first guy's neck, fast. No hesitation. None. He held the other one by his hair and landed a single chop to the base of the guy's skull. The guy in the middle, the big one— he took longer with him. I'm pretty sure he was the one who dropped the *n*-bomb. He talked to him for only a couple minutes, a brief conversation. Then the smaller guy pounded on him, punching and kicking. He looked into the guy's eyes and closed his hands around his throat. It was scary, Cap.

"When the smaller one finished, he cleaned out their pockets, got to his feet, and surveyed the alley. I checked my watch. It was almost midnight.

"'Shit,' I said. I whispered it.

"The guy turned and stared right in my direction. *Don't come this way*, I thought. *Please, please, please, don't come this way.* I closed my eyes. When I opened them, he was gone.

"Part of me, a real small part of me, wanted to go see about the other three guys, but they weren't moving. I remembered something my grandmother used to say. 'Ain't my circus, ain't my monkeys.' I thought about going to a pay phone to call the cops, but then I'd have been out there all night, and my grandmother would have had a stroke.

"I stood up and took a last look at the three dead guys in the alley. I knew I had class early the next morning. I walked out of the alley and didn't look back. All I cared about was how angry my grandmother would be at me. When I got home, she was fast asleep. Soon, so was I."

The detective, Earnest Cleaveland, sat back in his chair.

"What are you telling me?" Captain Askew asked.

The detective pointed to the file box on the table next to the captain's desk. He opened it and rifled through the pages. He pulled out pictures of the victims and the killer.

"I'm telling you, based on this article this morning, the guys who started this whole thing were those three guys." He pointed at pictures of the victims. "And I'm pretty sure—no, I'm certain—the guy who finished it was . . . well, we know who he was."

His boss stared at him.

"How certain are you?"

"One hundred percent, Cap," he said. "I was there." The captain stood, collected the file, and put it back into the file box. He put the box in the detective's hands.

"Let's go, Detective. We need to brief the chief."

Chapter 1

Bobby yawned while his agent reminded him of the obligations written into his current three-book deal with his publisher. He scrolled his phone while waiting for his flight in the United Airlines lounge at Southwest Florida International Airport in Fort Myers.

"That agreement you signed was actually a contract, Bobby," Doug Soskin said. Doug had been Bobby's agent since his first crime fiction novel, *The Laughing Killer*, was published by Bellingham thirteen years earlier. "They're expecting something from you they can count on. It's the way things are done in this business. But you already know all that."

It had been nearly three years since Bobby's last book hit the shelves. A long time, based on Bobby's record.

"Just for my own edification, Doug," Bobby began, with only the slightest trace of annoyance in his voice. "Have any of these folks ever written one—never mind six—best sellers? Do they think these things just happen because there's a contract in place? Do they not understand how a book gets put together by an author?"

"Okay, what's going on, Bobby?" Doug asked. "Really, you've never come close to missing a deadline before. I don't want to ask if you're blocked because neither one of us believes in that writer's block bullshit. Is there something else going on?"

Bobby was a very successful author in a very crowded, very competitive publishing space. His own publisher had nine equally prolific authors who wrote the same genre of books as Bobby—or Robert L. Kaminsky, as it appeared on the cover of his books.

Some authors can crank out a book a year. Some take two, even three years between titles. Some require more research. Some have higher standards and expectations, either on the part of the publisher or for themselves. But it really doesn't matter what the reasons are for one author's output versus that of another. Publishers get to make demands because they're the ones paying the six-figure advances.

"You know, Doug," Bobby began. "I'm not gonna insult you with excuses. Technically, I haven't missed the deadline yet. And I probably won't. They're just anxious. Honestly, I don't have a story that's up to my own standards right now, never mind theirs. I'll be in New York later today, and I'll be at the meeting at 2:00 p.m. tomorrow. We'll just have to see how things play out. We've had the conversation. You know as well as I that most publishers don't really give a rat's ass what's on the pages as long as the fans line up and buy whatever carries that author's name. I'm not one of those who write the same book over and over again. That hasn't been me for over a dozen years and a half-dozen titles. I'm not going to start writing like that now just to please Bellingham Books. If they want to void us because I'm not ready, we'll find another house."

"It's not going to come to that," Doug said. "Let's have the meeting tomorrow, see what comes out of it. We'll go from there. Are you sure I can't talk you into dinner at Luger's tonight?"

"No need. I have some things I want to noodle on a little, and rich food and drink isn't on that agenda. I'll be there tomorrow at 2:00 p.m. See you soon, buddy."

Bobby let out a long, exasperated sigh. *He's right*, Bobby thought. Something will shake loose soon, and he'll be on his way to bestseller number seven. He unfolded his rolled-up newspaper and tried to fill his head with something other than the blank screen on his computer and in his head.

• • •

Bobby missed the news brief when it was printed the first time, as it was buried on *USA Today*'s state-by-state page. It was under Pennsylvania, titled, "Supreme

Court Declines to Hear Final Appeal of Garrett Bensen."

> Confessed triple murderer Garrett Bensen was convicted in the killing of three people in August of 1992 in Harrisburg, Pennsylvania.
>
> He was captured in December 1993, tried in 1994, and sentenced to die by lethal injection. With no appeals remaining, Bensen will be executed at the State Correctional Institution in Greene County, Pennsylvania, on September 12, 2016.

Less than three months.

It wasn't Bobby's authorial eye that registered anomalies in the story—it was his close-to-the-surface emotional self.

First, the Garrett Bensen he knew was from Minnesota, not Pennsylvania. Second, the Garrett Bensen he knew could not be a killer, never mind what the paper referred to as a triple murderer.

Garrett Bensen had been Bobby's roommate in Germany thirty-four years earlier. He had movie star–level good looks. He was the one with whom Bobby had shared a near-death experience. He was self-effacing, shy, couldn't hold his liquor, and a God-awful pinochle player. But Garrett Bensen, a triple murderer? No. Not on any day, ever.

• • •

In 1981, Bobby Kaminsky was assigned to a small unit attached to a US Army base in a town not far from Frankfurt, in what was then referred to as West Germany. Their top-secret US Air Force outpost was housed on a restricted, well-guarded corner of the standby infantry base. Over time, the troops became a fraternity of sorts. When they weren't working, they were raising hell, either in Frankfurt or in Amsterdam or in some other town that had to put up with their post-adolescent, testosterone-driven, seemingly unending pursuit of women and beer.

Besides Bobby Kaminsky (called "Cityboy" because he was from Brooklyn), there was Johnny "Farmboy" Lee, Cleveland "Fatboy" Allebaugh, Bill "Cowboy" Densmore, and lastly, Garrett "Prettyboy" Bensen. Despite being entrusted with a top-secret mission involving national security, they were teenagers, barely young men. After an especially messy visit to Amsterdam when all but one of them followed three drunk Canadian Army guys into one of the city's dirtiest, smelliest, most polluted canals, Fatboy (the sensible one who stayed dry) dubbed the crew "the Filthy Five."

• • •

Until Bobby saw the *USA Today* blurb about Bensen, he hadn't thought about those guys in a long time.

With an hour remaining before he'd board his flight, Bobby parked himself in a quiet corner of the United

Airlines lounge, logged onto his laptop, and googled "Garrett Bensen." Up popped stories and images from every stage of Garrett's adult life, including his last state-mandated appeal.

Bobby shook his head. He tried to whistle but his mouth was dry. Even with over three decades in the rearview mirror, he recognized Prettyboy's younger face, especially those blue eyes. The account of what he did was horrifying. Bobby tried but couldn't get his head around Garrett Bensen wreaking all that havoc. All he could think was, *what the fuck happened to this kid?*

• • •

In a busy corner office at the state capitol building in Harrisburg, Pennsylvania, Senator Ed Ianucci closed his newspaper, planted a smug smile on his face, and sat back in his leather chair.

"I can't believe those *USA Today* assholes didn't include the name of the prosecutor. We're at the stage of the campaign where national publicity can only help us."

"You'll get plenty of press when we execute him," said Tom Cavanaugh, Ianucci's chief of staff.

"Yeah, I suppose." He sat up and clapped his hands twice. "Soon as we waste this piece of shit Bensen, we'll kick the campaign into high gear."

Cavanaugh shook his head. "We shouldn't get ahead

of ourselves, sir. A lot can happen between now and September twelfth."

Ianucci smiled. "I know you're just being cautious, Tommy, but this particular train left the station a long time ago." He rapped his knuckles on the desk. "It's preordained. Everything's moving ahead just as it should. Have I ever let you down? Ever?"

"No, sir. You haven't." Cavanaugh lifted his coffee cup. "To the next governor of Pennsylvania!"

They clinked cups. Ianucci's had a splash of cognac in it. "Salute!"

• • •

Garrett Bensen was the last and youngest to join the gang of airmen who became the Filthy Five. He'd gained membership by virtue of being Bobby's room-mate, but he was awarded bonus points because they all agreed that his adorable David Cassidy–like looks would serve as a magnet for attracting the ladies. He was that good looking. He was also just a really good kid.

Bobby pulled the name and contact info for Gar-rett's appellate lawyer from one of the news stories and placed a call to one Albert McCarthy in Mt. Lebanon, Pennsylvania.

"Who'd you say you are?" McCarthy asked.

"My name's Bob Kaminski." Back in the day every-one had called him Bobby. "I served with Garrett

Bensen in the air force in the early 1980s. I'd like to visit him before—"

"You write books?" McCarthy interrupted. Bobby smiled. It always pleased him when he came across someone who knew his work. Even with a healthy handful of titles, a couple of them actual best sellers, he was always surprised.

"Yes, I do, and thanks for asking."

"Why do you want to visit him?"

Okay, Bobby thought, *enough with the niceties.*

"I'm not sure what I hope to accomplish, Mr. McCarthy."

"Pennsylvania doesn't encourage visits to death-row inmates other than immediate family," McCarthy said.

"Honestly, sir, I'm not overly concerned with what they encourage or discourage," Bobby said. "Is it possible for me to visit with him? I'm able to come whenever you say."

"Let me be honest, Mr. Kaminsky. The prosecutor, Ed Ianucci, is a real tight ass when it comes to this case. Even though he won, and even though Bensen appealed out, he still throws high and tight at me anytime I ask for anything on this client's behalf. He's got a real hair up his ass about it."

"Mr. McCarthy," Bobby started.

"Call me Al."

"Al. Whoever this guy Ianucci is, he means less than nothing to me," Bobby said. "For your sake and Garrett's, I promise I'll tread lightly."

"All right. Call me in a couple of days."

Bobby still had almost an hour before his flight would be called. He set to locating the current whereabouts of the rest of the Filthy Five.

. . .

Johnny Lee grew up on a dairy farm due north of Durham, North Carolina, near the Virginia state line. Google led Bobby to the North Carolina Dairy Farmers Association in Raleigh. Listed in their membership directory were three operators named Lee, but only one Johnny Dale Lee. Johnny, not John. He punched in the number.

"JDL Dairies," announced a woman with a pleasant southern voice. "What can we do for you this beautiful summer day?"

Bobby smiled. He asked if Mr. Lee was available. She said he could choose from Johnny or John Junior.

"I'm looking for the one in his mid-to-late fifties."

"Well darlin', that means you are looking for Mr. Johnny Lee, Chairman, President, CEO, and all-around top bull here at Lee Dairies. May I tell him who is calling? Or would you prefer to just scare the living daylights out of him?"

Bobby chuckled.

"I don't want to give the top bull a heart attack. Please tell him it's Bobby. Bobby Kaminski."

"Hang on a minute, Bobby," she said. The recorded hold message enumerated the health benefits of wholesome, full-strength, Vitamin D milk. A moment later, a familiar voice boomed in Bobby's ear.

"This cannot possibly be goddamn Cityboy Bobby Kaminsky from goddamn Brooklyn, New York, now can it?"

"I see you still have that great gift with the English language," Bobby laughed. "This is indeed Bobby K. from Sheepshead Bay, Farmboy. Tell me, how're you doing this fine summer day, young man?"

They went through a minute or two of "how are you," and "where are you," and "what have you been up to" until Bobby got to the point of the call.

"So, what do you think about Prettyboy?" Bobby asked.

Farmboy exhaled. "I ain't even heard Prettyboy's name in—What is it?—thirty-some years? What's going on with him?"

"You don't know?"

"You talkin' about your old roommate, right?"

Bobby told him what he knew. His old roommate, their friend from those wild times, was going to die in September for killing three people in Pennsylvania in 1989.

"What kinda nonsense you tellin' me?" he asked. "Prettyboy killed three people? Come on, no way."

"I've got it right here in front of me, man," Bobby said. "I just got off the phone with his lawyer."

"Well, ain't that some kinda shit." he said. "If I had to

pick one of us to end up a killer, that would have been you, Bobby. Y'know, you bein' from Brooklyn and all."

"You have any idea what could have happened there?" Bobby asked.

"No sir, I don't," he said. "I'm not sure I really want to know, you know? I'd rather remember Prettyboy the way we knew him, way back when."

"I hear you. You in touch at all with Cowboy or Fatboy?" Bobby asked.

"No," he said, a tinge of melancholy in his voice. "I ain't heard hide nor hair from either of them. I'm sorry to say it, but they ain't heard from me neither."

It's true, Bobby thought. *Out of sight, out of mind.*

"If I remember right, they went home, I don't know, eight months, maybe almost a year after you left," Johnny said. "I re-upped and got shipped back to the States. I guess Prettyboy was on his own after that."

Farmboy said he stayed in for twenty before retiring at forty-five on a master sergeant's pension. He returned home and took over operation of the family dairy farm from his aging parents.

Bobby told him he wanted to visit real soon and would bring some authentic German beer when he did. Farmboy said Bobby was more than welcome, that he'd leave the farm with as much authentic, wholesome, North Carolina milk as he could carry.

Chapter 2

Bobby didn't have any trouble locating Bill Densmore—a.k.a. Cowboy, although Bobby had his doubts as to whether he'd ever been in any real proximity to either cows or horses. Tall and broad-shouldered with rugged good looks, Cowboy was the first-born son of William W. "Big Bill" Densmore, owner of the Densmore Foods Company, which had been headquartered along I-20 between Midland and Odessa in the desert middle of West Texas. Ten years before he sold the company to a massive food conglomerate, Big Bill moved the headquarters of Densmore Foods to Colorado and began planting the seeds for a second career in politics.

Former mayor of Denver and then senator from Colorado, Big Bill had big plans for his eldest son. That all changed when Cowboy got himself entangled with a stunning German girl. All Bobby remembered was her name: Monika.

They lost touch after Bobby got out of the service. Cowboy and Monika tied the knot in Munich after Oktoberfest in 1984. That little impulse cost Bill Densmore his security clearance and a boatload of family money, but as was always the case with Cowboy, he ultimately landed on his feet.

• • •

Bobby's flight began to board. He was leaving his home in Naples, Florida, for New York to meet with his editor and literary agent. Bobby's success as a novelist offered him the means and opportunity to chase down a little personal history if he so chose. The tiny seed of an idea began taking root in his brain.

• • •

When he got to the St. Regis, Bobby googled William Earle Densmore. Earle was his mother's maiden name—the Densmore's were that kind of family. He found Cowboy on a web site for a boutique New Mexico law firm, Densmore Borgen. The Borgen turned out to be Monika Borgen-Densmore. It appeared that after the air force, Bill and Monika settled in the States. They both attended college and then went on to law school. He dialed the number.

"Densmore Borgen. This is Abby. May I help you?"

"Hi, Abby. My name is Bob Kaminski. I'm calling for Bill Densmore."

"Does he know what this is in reference to?" she asked.

"He does not. But there's a chance he'll recognize my name."

"One moment, please."

Bobby laughed out loud at the hold button music, a German beer hall song. When the music stopped, all he could hear was laughter.

"Bobby Kaminski! What, are you in jail here in Santa Fe?" Cowboy always believed everyone wanted something from him. Apparently, nothing had changed in that regard.

"Actually, I'm calling to finally tell you the truth, Cowboy."

"Can't wait, Cityboy."

"You know that '82 gold Chevy of yours? The one your daddy sent over to Bremerhaven? I'm sorry, but that was one righteous piece of shit car." They both burst into laughter. "How's life, dude?"

"Life here in the foothills is outstanding. Let me guess. You're really calling about Prettyboy."

"Yeah. I just found out. I broke it to Farmboy yesterday. What do you know?"

He let out a deep sigh.

"Just that some time ago—late '80s if I recall correctly—he killed three men: a cop, an ex-cop, and some small-time dirt bag in Harrisburg, Pennsylvania, of all places. Apparently, the prosecutor tried to hang three other open homicides on him, but the trial judge threw them out." He sighed, remembering. The information about the three other homicides was news to Bobby.

"He reached out when he was caught," Cowboy said. "But I had a plateful up in Colorado Springs. Do you know about me after the air force?"

"I know you married Monika and fell out of favor with the family," Bobby said. "Seeing that piece in the paper yesterday made me realize how wrong I was not to keep in touch with guys who were so important to me back then."

"Ah, don't be hard on yourself, man. We all left that time behind. Hell, I haven't even talked to Fatboy in . . . Must be twenty-some-odd years. And you know how close we were." He paused, interrupted by something on his end. "Hey, where are you, Bobby? I need to call you back."

Bobby gave his number. He couldn't believe Cowboy and Fatboy had fallen out. They were the leaders of the crew. Densmore typically set the agenda; Fatboy managed logistics. The others, including Bobby, were happy passengers.

For the time, and considering the fact they were still kids, the Filthy Five had been a relatively sophisticated operation. Cowboy and Fatboy were roommates, as were Prettyboy and Cityboy. Farmboy's roommate in Germany was a non-commissioned officer. He was never invited to join the crew. When they were on their own time, the Filthy Five did not fraternize with management.

Bobby googled Fatboy's name and wasn't surprised to find him working in real estate in California, up in the Bay Area. Back in the day, it was the family business. Fatboy always said the world isn't making any more land, that when he got out, he was going to, as he put it, "get back into the dirt business." It was a little after three in the afternoon, California time. Bobby dialed the number.

"CW."

"CW? What the hell is a CW?" Bobby asked. "I thought this number belonged to a dirt merchant named Fatboy."

There was no pause on the other end of the line.

"Ooookay, now let's see. This isn't Cowboy, or Farmboy, and it damn sure isn't Prettyboy." He chuckled. "Holy shit, how the hell are you, Bobby?"

It amazed Bobby that people can be out of touch for so long, and still, all that time and space can evaporate like an afternoon rain shower in southwest Florida. They caught up, laughed about a couple of memories. Then Bobby bit the bullet and asked him about Prettyboy.

"You know, I always thought if one of us was going to get in trouble, it would be you or me, not the others," he said. "Never Prettyboy. He wasn't a scrapper. Well, except for that one time."

"Oh yeah, right," Bobby said. He'd forgotten about that one time.

• • •

May 1983

The beating took place four months into Prettyboy's membership in the crew. Following a solo trip to the Big Dog, a local Darmstadt *gasthaus* the Five considered home base, he stumbled back into their room really messed up. All of them at one time or another drank too much or mixed too much bratwurst and sauerkraut with too much Pfungstadter or St. Pauli Girl. Sometimes they threw up. Sometimes they fell. Sometimes they did both, but the Filthy Five didn't get into fights. Densmore always said the Five were lovers, not fighters.

Prettyboy had been professionally pummeled. When he came in at three in the morning, all he wanted was privacy and time. Bobby gave him both—but first thing in the morning, he talked with the others.

"I don't know what happened or who did it or even how bad he's hurt," he told them. "All I know is he's a mess and he's not talking about it."

"We need to get him to the dispensary so he can get patched up," Allebaugh said.

"We also need him to file a report with the APs so they can find out who did it," added Densmore. "Then we need to go kick somebody's ass."

"I just can't see what he could've done that someone would want to beat him so bad," said Johnny Lee. "He's a sweet kid."

"Yeah," Bobby said. "Sometimes his good looks and sweet nature gets him in trouble with jealous boyfriends. Plus, he's an easy mark for a bully."

The crew covered for Prettyboy at work so he could heal, but he still didn't give up anything about what actually happened. He asked them to give him some room. He said he didn't know who jumped him.

Everyone they knew went to the Big Dog at one time or another. It was friendly, the prices were good, and the waitress, Charlotte, offered a glimpse of what women in heaven must look like. Prettyboy said two guys stopped him on his way home after closing time. One held him while the other worked him over.

"They didn't say much, just pounded on me. It was dark and I was drunk, so no sense in going to the apes," he said. "Apes" is what air force guys called the air police—APs.

"Just give me a couple more days and I'll be me again," he promised.

It took a couple more weeks before he got his face back. Except for a broken rib and peeing a little blood, he returned to full Prettyboy status. Soon, they forgot what happened.

• • •

June 2016

Bobby gave Allebaugh his contact information and told him it wouldn't be thirty years before they talked again.

• • •

Robert Louis Kaminsky was the youngest child and only son of David and Elsie Kaminsky. He grew up in his parents' apartment in the Sheepshead Bay neighborhood of Brooklyn until he enlisted and left home for good.

This neighborhood was the White ethnic soup of lower middle-class Brooklyn. He played stickball and Ringolevio on safe streets and was able to take advantage of a then-outstanding public school education. His father gambled, mostly on horses, and his mother worked as a bookkeeper in Manhattan to help offset his chronic losses.

Bobby was a shy, inhibited kid with a much older sister and parents who, in their late forties at his birth, were genuinely surprised with his arrival on the scene. His father was ambivalent; he'd pictured a different kind of middle age for himself and Elsie. The scale was balanced by powerful, unconditional love on the part of Bobby's mother. Elsie desperately wanted a second child and was thrilled when she learned she was pregnant with Bobby and a twin. She miscarried Bobby's brother in her sixth month.

Bobby didn't enjoy his ordinary adolescence. He got by but never excelled, either academically or athletically. The one thing he did well was dream up and write down stories. He read everything he could get his hands on. He loved New York's public libraries, especially the big ones at Grand Army Plaza in Brooklyn and the main branch on Fifth Avenue at E. 42nd Street.

The high school years were not the best time in Bobby's life. Sheepshead Bay High School was very big and there were social castes and cliques he never understood and never cared to penetrate. He got through but didn't have the grades or the financial resources to go to any of New York City's public colleges without working a full-time job. No girlfriend, no tight circle of friends. Consequently, he wasn't sure what he'd do following his march across the stage at Loew's Kings Theater in June of 1979, after he collected his high school diploma. His after-school job working in the mailroom at a Wall Street brokerage firm didn't feel like anything special or something he wanted to pursue.

His father pressed Bobby to move out after his eighteenth birthday. He was the one who suggested his son look into military service. Not too many Jewish kids enlisted back then, but Bobby talked to a recruiter and learned that he could find some interesting work in the air force. What the recruiter laid out for him ensured he'd get to do some overseas travel. He wasn't sure at the time exactly why that prospect appealed to him. When he got out, he was promised nearly free college under the GI Bill.

Thirty-three days after collecting his diploma, Bobby Kaminsky left for basic training in San Antonio, armed with a toothbrush, two changes of underwear, a few other personal items, and a handful of blank journals. The journals were his mother's idea. Like a baby growing in the womb, Bobby found himself re-born nine months later in Darmstadt, West Germany, attached to a top-secret intelligence unit monitoring and intercepting communication between targeted Warsaw Pact military installations. It was the time of Ronald Reagan in the US and Yuri Andropov in the Soviet Union. No one really knew or could even imagine what might happen with those two in charge of nuclear weapons.

He filled all nine of the journals during his first six months in West Germany. He didn't know it at the time, but he was well on his way to his future career as an author.

• • •

Bobby returned home from his business trip and briefed his wife, Lindy, on what he'd learned about his friends from long ago.

"So, these guys are real," she said, smiling. "I thought they were creatures of that fertile imagination of yours."

"Very real," he said. "It's hard to believe how much time has passed."

"A triple murder, huh?"

Bobby just shook his head. "I can't get my head around that."

"What's on your mind?"

Lindy was Bobby's best friend, his occasional muse,

and the buzz saw through the mass of bullshit residing in the space between his ears.

"I think . . ." He paused. "I'm going to take a little road trip."

Lindy nodded.

"Good idea. Take copious notes," she said. "Who knows? If nothing else, there might be a book here."

He smiled.

"I don't know, Lin. Fiction has been good to us. I'm not sure I can really do facts."

She sat down at the dining room table, a signal that he should join her for a serious talk.

"You're an idiot, you know."

"Wow!" Bobby laughed. "That's encouraging. Thanks, honey."

She laughed and shook her head.

"Bobby," she began. "You've been doing this writing thing for a long time. By any measure, you've gotten to a point where your publisher, if they're as smart as you tell me they are, will look at what you've done and give you wide berth."

Bobby's insecurities always came as a surprise to Lindy. Since they'd been together, eighteen years now, she always held him in higher regard than he did himself. Why, after he'd done so much so well, she had no idea.

"I'm going to visit with these guys, visit Garrett and talk to his attorney. After that, I should be able to figure out if there's a book there. But just so you know, this is a whole lot less about me doing another book and a whole lot more about me having to understand what the hell happened to this kid."

Lindy put her arms around him. This was a second marriage for them both. He'd jettisoned the dead weight of his first marriage. Yes, there were two daughters. Yes, he loved them both unconditionally. He stayed as present in their lives as much as they wanted him to.

When Lindy Mason arrived on his scene like a comet from deep space, she cratered a hole in his heart only she could fill. Everything good he did after that, he credited to the enormous bright light she shined into his life.

"My thoughts exactly," she said. "Now get going."

• • •

Bobby called Johnny Lee to gauge if now was a good time for a visit.

"Just don't come too early in the morning or late in the afternoon," Farmboy said. Something about having to get several hundred dairy cows—"his girls"—to surrender their treasure.

Bobby threw two bags into his Subaru Outback early the next morning and began the nine-hundred-mile drive from Naples to the JDL Dairy Farm in Blakesville, North Carolina.

• • •

The Lee family farm was established in the late 1890s, at which time it constituted a bit more than forty acres, two mules, and a few Holsteins, plus Uncle Joe, the lone bull. By the time Johnny came along in 1959, Lee Dairy Farms was nearly eight hundred acres, over two hundred highly productive "girls," and a fledgling processing and private-label cheese operation.

Johnny's family was deep into the local community. Johnny grew up with two older brothers, neither of whom had any interest in dairy farming, and parents that worked hard, drank, and danced on Saturday nights, then woke up early Sunday morning to worship God and Jesus in the Blakesville Reformed Baptist Church. When the time came for him to slip off, Johnny Lee would be laid to rest within ten miles of the very spot where he was born.

Seven days each week, as he morphed from skinny kid into rock solid man, Johnny hand milked two, sometimes three, dozen of the girls. When vacuum bucket milking arrived on the scene, he'd come far enough along to oversee the growing dairy's entire production operation.

In his junior year of high school, through no overt action of his own, John caught the attention of the young ladies. It was 1977, four short years before he'd move from farmhand to Deutschland. Johnny was seeing a gaggle of local gals. Each of them, after two or three visits to the drive-in movie theaters, set out to put all the others out of the Johnny Lee business. At first, Johnny couldn't understand it. He was sufficiently self-aware to know he wasn't rich or overly good looking or captain of the football team or student class president. He was having fun until things started to get serious and complicated. Johnny Lee did not like serious or complicated, especially when it came to young ladies.

His daddy told him not to get too attached.

"Sooner or later, each one of them will be gone. Then whatcha gonna do, boy?"

Johnny's self-awareness didn't include any real idea as to how growing up a Lee in the small community—farms and faith were the dominant attributes—sometimes got translated to others in similar, if not quite as impressively influential circumstances. His own family never talked about how theirs was on track to become perhaps one day the largest dairy operation in the entire state, or that how Johnny was on track to one day become the owner-operator of said large and profitable enterprise. This evaluation didn't pass unnoticed among the parents of young women in the community, who unashamedly encouraged their daughters to do their best to get to know this, potentially, at least, future agribusiness leader.

But it was hard letting go of these notions and attachments. These gals had been well-educated by their own families regarding Johnny's special status, and each of them did whatever they needed to do to try to keep him corralled within the confines of a community with a very strong overall component involving faith.

Right before he snuck off to save his skin and serve his country, he severed all potentially romantic ties with the girls, leaving himself free to explore all the possibilities before him, at least for the next four years.

Eventually, following his return home after his first enlistment and his Filthy Five days, he met Shelby Staples, a young transplant to Blakesville from Charleston, South Carolina. Shelby had no other agenda than her deep affection for him. She declared ownership of his heart and the rest, including sixteen more years in Uncle Sam's Air Force, is family history, family business, and life.

Chapter 3

After an overnight at an Embassy Suites outside Savannah and then seven more hours of interstates and rural two-lanes, Bobby pulled through the gates of Johnny Lee's operation around 3:00 p.m. He had no idea what to expect but it was evident Farmboy had clearly done well for himself. After a quarter-mile drive past pastures cluttered with more plump dairy cows than he could count, Bobby arrived at a small compound contained within a white picket fence.

Inside the fence were two houses and a sprawling single-story, flat-roofed building.

One of the houses turned out to be a residence, a white, two-story antebellum with a wraparound front porch and Doric columns where Johnny and his family lived. The other house, a wide, low-slung, dark-red-and-pale-yellow, midcentury modern ranch, contained the administrative offices of JDL Dairies, Inc. Nearby was a vast, interconnected array of Quonset huts with a distribution deck behind, where products carrying the JDL logo were processed, bottled, packaged, and shipped. In addition to all the real estate, dairy cows, and JDL team members, the business operated a fleet, as Bobby later learned, of eighty-five refrigerated delivery trucks that filled the dairy cases of supermarkets and convenience stores throughout the American South.

Bobby approached the ranch first, letting himself in through the blue front door leading into the office suite. There, a small, naturally lit foyer, two upholstered armchairs, a coffee table covered with trade magazines, and two planters with lush weeping figs. Family photographs going back generations filled all available wall space. The foyer emptied into a large room, where the top bull himself, Johnny Lee, leafed lazily through a *Wall Street Journal*. Perched in an old slat-backed desk chair, his Tony Lamas rested on a stack of papers atop the wooden desk. A black beaver-hide Stetson cocked back on his head. He chewed on a fat, unlit cigar.

Seeing Bobby, Farmboy leaped to his feet and removed his hat, revealing a lush mane of salt-and-pepper hair—more salt than pepper. He set the cigar in an ashtray, put a huge smile on his tan, clean-shaven face, and met Bobby with a hug that stole his breath.

"God damn, it's good to see you, Cityboy!" he said. "Welcome to the family business. You want some milk?"

A woman at the front desk (where the actual work

seemed to be done) smiled, hurried over, and gave Bobby a hug.

"I'm Shelby, Johnny's old lady for the past thirty-one years. It's good to meet you, Mr. Kaminski."

"Hi, Shelby," he said. "Please, call me Bobby."

"Johnny's always talked about y'all, but you're the first livin' and breathin' one I ever met. I figured he'd made up all that Filthy Five nonsense. We talked on the phone last week. I and some of the other ladies do the work that doesn't involve emptying cow udders."

Farmboy introduced Bobby to his two sons, John Junior, the chief operating officer of JDL, and young Dale, still in school at Duke. After he graduated, Dale would no doubt join his brother in the family business. Farmboy had built himself a beautiful family and, from all appearances, a thriving business.

That night, over a long dinner involving outrageously delicious fried chicken, butterbeans, sweet potato pie, and a twelve-pack of the imported Lowenbrau Bobby had brought, the family stayed up 'til two in the morning reliving a few, mostly G-rated stories from the Filthy Five's history book.

Bobby did the math; if Johnny and Shelby had been married for thirty-one years, that meant he connected with her right after he rotated to the States, sometime in the mid-1980s. He'd never mentioned a girlfriend when they were running together, which was good as Johnny Lee had a singular reputation when it came to the *frauleins*. Neither of them brought up a favorite episode that occurred in Amsterdam in early 1981, before Bensen had joined the crew.

• • •

March 1981

Bobby was on leave the day President Reagan got shot. After calling his CO to make sure personal leaves hadn't been canceled, he tried but was unable to locate Densmore or Allebaugh. Johnny Lee was happy to catch a train from Frankfurt to meet Bobby in Amsterdam. Farmboy had three free days that matched with Bobby's last days of leave, so the plan was to play around some, then head back to base.

They met at the Central Station just in time to join the Queen's prayer vigil in the Dam Square that was being held for the President. Bobby estimated there were a hundred thousand people assembled to pray for Mr. Reagan. Neither Bobby nor Johnny spoke Dutch, other than what was necessary, but small American flags waved all over the packed square. They heard Reagan's name mentioned enough times to make an educated guess regarding the contents of her address.

Afterward, they headed to the Happy House, their preferred A-dam inn near Rembrandt Square. The Happy House featured a small bar, unambitious restaurant, and four stories with a dozen or so rooms up a narrow, winding staircase. The owners, brothers Benny and Tommy, acted as concierges for the inn's guests.

Whatever Bobby and Johnny wanted or needed, Benny or Tommy would round it up. Several in the crew stayed there maybe ten times in 1981 alone.

A Dutch girl, Joke, (pronounced 'yo-ka'), sat on a stool at the bar. She was short, maybe 5'2", and filled out anything she wore. She and Bobby shared pleasant history—he thought they might pick up where they'd left off the last time he was there—but she couldn't stop laughing at the enhanced version of Johnny's drawl, which he laid on extra thick when he was talking up a woman. Soon, Farmboy winked a "see you later" to Bobby and he and Joke headed upstairs, leaving Tommy and Bobby to talk about the assassination attempt on the American president.

Three days later, after Bobby had been pretty much on his own in Amsterdam, the hour approached for them to head back to Germany. Johnny was still MIA. Bobby didn't want to gamble on whether Johnny might or might not show up—they had a train to catch. Benny promised to track him down and get him on the next available train to Frankfurt, but they were set to work a midnight shift two hours after their scheduled return to base.

When Bobby got to the Central Station in Amsterdam, he spotted Johnny sitting on a bench with Joke unashamedly straddling his lap. Her skirt was hitched up around her midsection. For all Bobby knew, they were having sex right there in front of God and everyone. Johnny was whispering who knows what kind of nonsense into her ear. She sat, smiling, eyes wide, mouth open, taking it all in, nodding, kissing him. Bobby approached with caution. Farmboy took notice and smiled.

"Hey, Cityboy," he said. "Glad you could make it. Me and Yoker here had us a good old time, right, baby?" Joke, maintaining her silly smile, just nodded, never taking her eyes off him.

"Y'know, I think this here gal likes me," he said. They stood and locked lips and tongues before she reluctantly disengaged, got herself as together as she possibly could, and sashayed out of the station. Johnny laughed.

"So, you two took up for the whole three days?" Bobby asked him. "No food, no . . . shower?" he asked, taking in his friend's ripe aroma.

He smiled, patted Bobby on the head, and told him they'd had all they needed right there in his room at the Happy House.

"I tried to give her some money before we left. It's how she pays her bills, right?" he said. "But she wouldn't take none of it. Just kept coming back for more. Near wrung me out, Cityboy. We really gotta work tonight?"

They boarded the train for Frankfurt and caught a local transfer to Darmstadt. Johnny slept the sleep of the righteously exhausted for the entire six hours. They made their shift and shared the experience with the rest of the crew. Cowboy laughed out loud when

Farmboy told the tale of "Yoker" and sixty hours of sexual marathon debauchery.

"You didn't make her any promises, right, Farmboy?" Fatboy asked.

Farmboy smiled and shook his head. "We didn't really do a whole lot o' talkin'," Johnny said. "Way too busy, and besides, as y'all know, this here weren't my first rodeo."

• • •

June 2016

While they shared a lot with Johnny's family that night, at Cityboy's prompting, they didn't share that little nugget.

Chapter 4

The next day, Bobby drove back to Naples nursing a hangover headache when Garrett's lawyer, Al McCarthy, called. He'd arranged a visit. Bobby told him to lock it down. Was there anything he needed to know when he arrived at the maximum-security facility in Waynesburg?

"Senator Ianucci—he was the prosecutor on Bensen's case before jumping to the state senate—isn't at all thrilled about you coming," McCarthy said. "So don't expect too friendly a welcome at Waynesburg."

"Why's he still got his panties in a wad about Bensen?" he asked. "The guy is going to die soon. I just want to visit him, not break him out."

"Who knows?" McCarthy said. "Ianucci's running for governor. I guess he's concerned about anything that might tarnish his *tough-on-crime* image."

Bobby told the lawyer he looked forward to meeting him and hung up.

With a little luck, he'd get to visit Densmore and

Allebaugh before seeing Bensen and find out what went wrong after Bensen left the service.

• • •

Back home, Bobby amused Lindy with his report from JDL Dairies, did some research, and sketched out a few preliminary ideas in his notes file. The next morning, he caught a flight to San Francisco to reconnect with Fatboy.

Cleveland Washburn Allebaugh was the second of his name, but never fully embraced the title of "Junior." Born near the end of Ike's second term, his parents had called him CW from day one.

Young CW always felt like an outsider because of his weight. Born at nearly eleven pounds, he was a chubby kid until high school, when chubbiness gave way to just plain fat.

His father, himself a case study in corpulence, insisted CW wasn't fat: "You're just short for your natural weight," he'd say, thus CW didn't invest much effort in trimming down.

At Santa Monica High School in the mid-'70s, CW never had the same social pull as his peers. He was artistically creative and hypersensitive. He joined Thespians, the school's drama club, Colors, the school's drawing and painting program, and played French horn in the school's band.

For two years after high school, he worked as a paid intern in his father's real estate brokerage, where he learned the language and legal nuances of the business. He believed this would guide his career path once he dispensed with college, as his mother demanded.

CW was just shy of his twentieth birthday when he experienced a defining moment that required him to adjust his and his father's expectations about a career in real estate.

One day when CW was alone at his father's Rancho Palos Verdes office, a young man named Corey Elkins walked into Cleveland Washburn Realty. CW's father and the rest of the agents and brokers were out showing properties or trolling for listings.

Corey had just relocated from New York City and was looking for a place to live. Like so many other young transplants, Corey had his sights set on a career in film or television. He had the looks and the ambition to get himself in front of people who could make his dream a reality. Whether or not he had any talent wasn't readily apparent. But CW smelled an opportunity in this twenty-something male model looking to live near the epicenter of *the industry*. CW was ready to make an impression on both the client and his father.

CW was self-conscious about his weight but possessed an engaging sense of humor and a fundamental understanding of his father's expectations. He offered Corey a cup of coffee and a book of listings. Two hours later, CW and Corey left to scout out properties.

The two hit it off famously, which led to dinner

together, which led CW to finally understand why dates he'd gone on with girls didn't do it for him.

Corey found a townhouse in Venice that brought the young, unlicensed CW his first commission check—a princely sum of $2,480. But Corey also found someone else to help him accelerate his arrival onto the motion picture and television industry scene. Crushed, confused, and needing distance, CW enlisted in the air force. He lied and told his heartbroken parents he wanted to see the world before joining the family business.

But Bobby knew none of this when his plane landed at San Francisco International Airport.

• • •

Fatboy had told Bobby to meet him for drinks and dinner at a small Italian place in North Beach. Bobby's eyes scanned Pepino's dozen or so tables before settling on a shiny-headed, round-faced, clean-shaven, cherubic-looking guy wearing a black silk collared shirt over a pair of white slacks. When he stood up to greet him, Bobby saw that Fatboy was thinner, older of course, and more than just possibly gay. He hadn't seen that coming.

"Welcome, Cityboy, to the city by the bay," he said, hugging him. Then, pointing to a seat at a small four-top, "I can't tell you how good it is to see you."

There was a heaping tray of mussels bubbling in a concoction of garlic and butter atop a table burner, a jug of Chianti, a couple of glasses, and a long loaf of crusty bread. There were three settings at their table.

They took each other in for a moment. Fatboy shook his head.

"I know. You had no idea, right? Neither did Cowboy. When I finally told him, he stopped talking to me. In fact, it was on that same call when I learned about Bensen."

"That had to be a while ago, right?"

"Yeah, it was. A long time ago." Fatboy downed some melancholy, along with a healthy chug of Chianti.

Bobby considered the notion of whether people ever really know one another. Looking back, he was able to understand how in youth, relationships are either superficial or way, way too deep.

"Somehow, I'm not entirely surprised about his re-action," Bobby said. "We all know how he was back then. I hope he can get beyond it. Truth is, I had no clue when we were running together."

Fatboy smiled. Then he laughed.

"No clue? Really? Not even when you consider I never hooked up with any girls on any of our adventures?"

In hindsight, Bobby could easily connect the dots. They had been way too self-absorbed to notice how Fatboy didn't chase any of the women they encountered during their travels.

"There were at least half a dozen gay guys on our

flight in D-stadt," Fatboy said, ticking off a few names. A couple of the names mentioned were out, but others were just as closeted as CW had been. It was Bobby's turn to shake his head.

"No idea, man. And no issue here either."

"It's possible Prettyboy might have known but I can't be sure." Fatboy laughed. "I don't know if you ever learned this, but there was this one night in Frankfurt. You, Johnny, and Densmore were in Copenhagen . . ."

• • •

February 1983

There were a couple of places in Frankfurt that weren't outright gay bars but were managed in a way that met the needs of both the military and civilian gay populations. One weekend, Farmboy, Cowboy, and Cityboy were in the Danish capital. The Five didn't have a group agenda for that break.

Their work schedules involved rotating shifts—days, swings, and midnights. Six days on, two off, six on, two off, six on, three off. Most of the time they hung out together but occasionally they'd do separate things. Bobby played pinochle as part of a competitive floating game. Every now and then he'd stay behind for some marathon session that could last thirty-six hours before extreme fatigue, beer abuse, or temporary blindness set in.

Fatboy and Prettyboy were at the Barbie Doll Bar in Frankfurt. Prettyboy was deeply engrossed with a busty redhead, so Fatboy left and headed for a place he knew existed but had never been.

It was called the Martinskeller. It was a basement room with a low ceiling, a horseshoe-shaped bar in the center, and an average but noisy live band. Working girls, party girls, locals, and GIs all frequented the Keller. It was open all night. The beer and brats were reasonable, the girls were quite good looking, and the place was gay-friendly.

CW stayed late into the night and was surprised when Garrett stumbled in—literally. He was well on his way to falling-down drunk. The poor kid could never hold more than a couple of beers. It only took a moment before Emerald, a Martinskeller regular, zeroed in on the new catch. Allebaugh was with a new friend and caught sight of Bensen out of the corner of his eye.

Emerald was a forty-something of ambiguous gender. She had the outward appearance of a Greek-Irish goddess. Tall with long reddish-brown hair and a statuesque but no doubt heavily augmented body, full red lips, and wearing five-inch heels. She carried a rhinestone-studded purse. Her green-sequined, skin-tight dress was the color of her eyes. She was impossible to ignore. Some had opined that Emerald was the inspiration for the Kinks' song, "Lola." She'd been around for a while.

Drunk as he was, Garrett hit Emerald with that thousand-watt smile of his. Emerald returned the favor. Before he could react, she took his hand and walked him onto the dance floor. It was a slow song. With high heels, she was taller than him. She clutched Garrett to her, his body flush against hers. It didn't take long before he realized that things weren't exactly as they first appeared.

Garrett was incapable of reacting in any way other than politely. Emerald was not accustomed to nice GIs. Most of the American men who fooled around with her either understood who she was and wanted to go there or understood who she was and played with cruel intent. Prettyboy was the un-GI, a wide-open book. He started coughing and disengaged.

Fatboy was close enough to hear him.

"Please, excuse me, I'm—I have something caught in my throat," he stammered.

Emerald smiled at him, but she knew. Garrett wasn't even out the door before she'd IDed her next enterprise.

Fatboy saw Prettyboy coming and going. He promised himself not to rag on the kid. Fatboy didn't know that Garrett had also seen him, while he was dancing with an overweight gent who turned out to be a flag-level army officer. Likely, that was the true cause of Garrett's coughing fit. He never said a word to any of the rest of the Five, and neither did Fatboy.

• • •

June 2016

"Nope," Bobby said, dabbing at his eyes from having laughed so much at Allebaugh's telling. "Didn't know about that."

"Well, now you do."

"So," Bobby said, reacquiring his bearings. "You got out, moved to 'Frisco, and came out?"

Fatboy laughed and signaled for the waiter. He ordered veal marsala, roasted eggplant, and crusty baked potatoes for both of them. He looked at his watch, a gold Raymond Weil, and told the server a third would be joining them and would he please keep another serving at the ready.

"I got out less than a year after you left for Turkey. It was probably before you were discharged. I went back to Orange County to work with my dad in the company's new commercial real estate business." He hesitated, then looked at Bobby and smiled. "I got married, had three kids, and lived the dream down in Costa Mesa."

Bobby's face fell into disarray. He had no idea what to do with that nugget.

Fatboy shrugged. "My dad had no idea, and I couldn't just drop it on him. Dad's business partner hooked me up with Sally. We got on famously, and I toughed it out until the world changed sufficiently so that I didn't have to stay in the shadows any longer. I must tell you, Bobby, Sally was, and still is, the most awesome woman I have ever known." He smiled, remembering.

"When I laid things out for her, she told me to follow my heart, that we'd both take care of the kids. As each one got old enough to understand, and as the world continued changing around us, we explained things to them. On that front, believe it or not, everything is just great."

"What about your dad? And your mom?" Bobby asked.

"Dad's gone. He died before Sally and I split so he never had to deal with it." He paused. "He and my mother divorced just before I left the service. I have no idea where she is."

He changed the subject and asked Bobby about his life. Bobby gave him the abridged version.

"When I came home from Turkey, I was twenty-two and unemployable."

Their air force skill set had very limited application beyond the military setting. Any related civilian jobs would have involved either NSA or CIA.

"I got married, moved from nothing job to nothing job for years, picked up two outstanding daughters along the way, and was looking forward to a painfully meaningless and boring existence. We moved from Queens to Florida for the sake of the girls and really struggled for a while."

Bobby had always enjoyed writing. After a year of

barely surviving, he got a break and went to work with a small, edgy advertising and public relations firm. There, he was able to flex his creative muscles and before long was writing radio and television ad copy, along with message platforms and talking points.

"In my off time I started writing for my own enjoyment," he said. "Mostly articles and columns for local magazines and trade publications, but also some short fiction."

"Not surprised," Fatboy said. "You always had a good imagination."

"A short story I wrote got published so I quit working, enrolled in college on the GI Bill, and started writing more or less full time," Bobby said. "You may recall my impulse control issues. My ex couldn't take the uncertainty of the writing life, so she split and took the girls. I sold some more stories, one of which got optioned and brought me a nice check. That story became a screenplay, which became a film, which made some money, which set me free to write without the pressure of wondering when I'd eat next."

"Wow," Fatboy said.

"Later, I got married again, this time to Lindy. She's a phenomenal gal who gets me and gives me the room to do what I do best," Bobby said. "Six books and two films later, here I am."

Fatboy ordered another bottle of Chianti and filled Bobby in on the intricacies of Bay Area commercial real estate. Then they got to Garrett Bensen.

"I still have difficulty processing this whole thing with Prettyboy," Allebaugh said. "None of what I've been told jives with the person we knew." He paused. "Not long after you left for Turkey, the crew fell apart. Densmore lost his clearance and all that family money. Farmboy re-upped early and got assigned stateside. Last I'd heard, he got married and became a lifer."

"I saw him last week," Bobby said. "He's running a sizable dairy operation in North Carolina and has an awesome family. Milking cows, packaging cheese, making money, and doing just fine."

"Nice," Fatboy said. "So, what's your deal? Is visiting the crew part of some bucket list or something?"

Bobby shook his head.

"Nope. After I read about Bensen, I decided to look you all up." He sipped his wine. It was good, better than anything he'd gotten in Florida. "I've always wondered what happened. We were so close. How does all that just stop, without so much as a holiday card?"

The front door of Pepino's opened. Early evening light washed in, along with a tall, well-dressed gent. He headed for their table. Allebaugh smiled, stood up, and hugged the guy.

"This is Mike Tomczak, my husband. Mike, say hello to Bobby Kaminsky, a.k.a. Cityboy, a treasured relic from a hundred years ago."

Mike extended a big hand and pulled Bobby out of his seat.

"I have heard so much over the years about CW's crew from Germany."

Mike was a San Francisco police detective who worked the Mission district of the city. He told Bobby he and Fatboy had been together for about twelve years. As soon as it became legal in California, they got married in a civil ceremony.

"Cityboy is in town for . . . How long are you here?" Allebaugh asked.

"Likely only tonight and part of tomorrow," Bobby answered. "I want to see if I can connect with Densmore before heading to Pennsylvania to see Prettyboy."

The server brought Mike his dinner and a third bottle of Chianti for the table. Bobby had a room at the Fairmont so he'd be able to sleep off the effects of the wine before heading to Santa Fe—if Densmore could fit him in.

"What do you hope to accomplish? Based on what you've told me, Prettyboy's going to die soon," Fatboy said.

"I don't know. I need to try to understand it all. Besides," Bobby said. "I might turn it into a story or a book or . . . I really don't know."

They ate in silence. Mike let out a long, deep sigh.

"Look," he said. "I only know what CW has told me about Garrett Bensen and what kind of group you guys were back then. But I do know something about people who kill other people. When they've confessed, been tried, convicted, and are appealed out, there usually isn't any good outcome. Especially in a state with capital punishment."

Bobby nodded and put a tight smile on his face. "Yeah, but when the person is someone you know—"

"Knew," interrupted Fatboy. "Someone you knew. A long time ago."

"You're right," Bobby said, pointing a finger at his friend, "But when you knew someone, the equation changes. At least for me. I lived with this kid for over a year. I worked with him and partied with him, and I really liked him. It's just part of my DNA to get a handle on what went wrong. Why would this sweet kid from Minnesota turn into the kind of person who could kill three people in cold blood in Pennsylvania? Besides, reconnecting with you guys at this crucial time in my life is worth the effort alone."

Fatboy and Mike smiled, accepting Bobby's passion. But he wasn't done yet.

"Look, I don't mean to get preachy, but I didn't know that Johnny Lee had a big dairy farm and a terrific family. I didn't know Fatboy was gay. I have no idea what may surface when I see Cowboy. I mean, who the hell could have imagined I'd be an author? Seriously. None of that matters or changes anything, but to me—that's important stuff. This is how I'm wired. Maybe I can't do anything for Garrett, but I need to know what happened to this kid."

"I hate to say it," Allebaugh said. "But it looks like he did what they said he did."

"Okay," Bobby said, putting on his devil's advocate hat. "Just for shits and grins. How do we really know? People confess to crimes they didn't commit all the time, right, Mike?"

"Yes, they do," Mike nodded. "But that's the exception. And a confession doesn't typically end with a death sentence."

Bobby filed that thought, but Mike had more to say.

"When CW told me that a friend from the air force was going to take the needle if his appeal was denied, I called a colleague in Pittsburgh. He reached out to someone in Harrisburg and got some insight, both into this case and into how things worked back there, back then," Mike said. "Bensen copped to three murders right after he was caught. A very aggressive, very ambitious DA, along with some higher-ups in the Harrisburg PD and at least one judge, wanted to clear some oldies. So they bundled in three unsolved cases."

"Bensen's lawyer is sending me a summary," Bobby said. "I'll go over the whole case file when I get to Pennsylvania."

They paused to finish dinner.

"Hey," Fatboy jumped in, changing the subject. "Remember the jackets?"

Bobby laughed. "Yeah, the jackets that never materialized. My fault for getting reassigned."

"What jackets?" Mike asked.

Bobby pointed to Allebaugh. "Your boy here wanted

the five of us to get jackets. Camelhair, if I remember right?"

"With a crest on the front breast pocket," Fatboy said.

"*Filthius Funfüs*," Bobby said. "With an umlaut over the second *u*."

"I also wanted the crest to show a beer stein, a fräulein, a castle, and a Volkswagen," Allebaugh added. They both smiled at the memory.

"We would have looked like some stupid, out-of-tune, doo-wop group," Bobby said. "I'm actually kind of sorry that never happened."

They finished their meals, their wine, and their stories. Bobby reached for the check, but Fatboy would have none of it. Bobby gave Mike a handshake and Fatboy a hug and promised he'd keep him looped. Mike, seeing Bobby just a little tipsy, drove him to the Fairmont, where he wished him a good night's sleep.

Chapter 5

Bobby indeed slept like a stone. The next morning, he checked out, called Densmore Borgen, and told the receptionist he was on his way to Santa Fe and that her boss needed to give him some non-billable time.

. . .

Bill Densmore's life had been planned for him before he was born into what constituted business and social royalty in West Texas. The family's business operation was food processing—canned vegetables, beans—but the family hobby was power, prestige, and politics. While he was growing up, young Billy was his daddy's pride and joy.

Big Bill, Densmore's father, took over the entire family business when his own father died from complications associated with liver disease. Young Bill spent his early childhood in a very exclusive, very White private school just off I-20 between Midland and

Odessa. The school was built on land donated fifty years earlier by Bill's grandfather, Denny Densmore, who didn't want any of his offspring burdened with a public-school education. He feared it might expose his fortunate sons to lesser Whites or, heaven forbid, Black or Latino kids. Bill's college prep experience included stints at a toney Dallas boarding operation, followed by a very brief visit to Phillips Academy in Andover, Massachusetts.

Young Bill didn't care for the boarding school experience. He didn't much care about school at all; with each successive grade, he got into more and more mischief.

Bill finished high school in precisely the environment his parents tried to avoid for him—among lesser beings undeserving to breathe the same rarefied air as these children of privilege. To youngsters of ordinary parentage, Central High School in Midland would have been a fine preparatory experience for a public university education, or job, or whatever worked for the other high school graduates at the time. But for the son of Big Bill Densmore, exposure to White trash, Jews, Catholics, Blacks, and Mexicans was deemed demeaning and inappropriate.

Bill couldn't, or wouldn't, help himself. He existed as a constant source of embarrassment for his mother and father. He didn't walk the stage at his graduation. As soon as he got his diploma, he went to work in the family's canning plant to learn the business from the bottom up. Bill knew that West Texas would have to exist without him representing the next generation of the Densmore dynasty.

His "bottom up" experience at Densmore Foods lasted two years, during which time he continued frustrating his family with a few public intoxication arrests, one quashed paternity charge from a Catholic Latina, and, in the shameful last straw for the boy, seriously dating the Jewish daughter of the upper-middle-class owners of two Odessa furniture stores. Big Bill told his son he needed to get his shit together or get the hell out of town. So young Bill visited an air force recruiter, and the rest was, to the consternation of his father, a most satisfying history.

• • •

Bobby flew into Albuquerque and rented a car for the ninety-minute drive to the Santa Fe offices of the Densmore Borgen law firm. It was situated on Johnson Street, diagonally across from the Georgia O'Keefe Museum. He promised himself a brief visit there after his business with Cowboy was finished.

The outer office at the Densmore Borgen firm was furnished in a strange mix of *L.A. Law*, American Southwest, and just a hint of Munich. The walls were painted a deep forest green. The artwork was Pueblo style. The rug on the hardwood floor featured browns and tans. The furniture was steel and glass with a sleek high-tech look.

White lettering on a black pole sign welcomed him, shouting *Bobby K. from Sheepshead Bay*. Bobby smiled. *Fucking Densmore*, he thought.

Abby, the receptionist, greeted Bobby warmly before depositing him in a well-appointed conference room. Bobby was impressed to note the Densmore Borgen firm had a dozen lawyers and an equal number of support staff all buzzing around in an active, noisy setting.

His eye settled on a placard hanging left of a window that looked out onto Johnson Street, where Bobby could see his rental car parked at a meter with two hours left on it. The placard was like one of those faux handmade wooden signs one might find in a Cracker Barrel. "Cowboys are always better than the other boys" it read in a white painted scrawl. That put another smile on Bobby's face.

A stunning middle-aged woman walked in carrying a silver tray, on which sat a tall pilsner glass of beer, a can of Diet Coke, and a steaming cup of tea. Monika Borgen-Densmore put the beer down in front of him, smiled, and took a seat. Bobby was mesmerized.

"My husband will be in after he finishes a call," she said. "I'm Monika, and you, I am told, are Cityboy?" Her English was flawless, and her smile was just as dazzling as he remembered. "Did we ever meet in Darmstadt?" she asked.

Bill Densmore had given up a lot for Monika Borgen. Most GI love affairs were measured in hours. This one had stood the test of time, going on now for over thirty years. Bobby stared at her. Beauty and brains, like his Lindy. He'd forgotten how gorgeous she was.

"Momentarily," he said. "The same night you met what's-his-name. You're only here because he had the good sense to move faster than the rest of us."

"Right," she said. "That was when Charlotte introduced us. I wonder what ever became of her."

"No idea," he said. "I hope your children favor you. Because, you know, your husband . . ."

"Yeah, yeah," Cowboy said, entering the room. He lightly smacked Bobby in the back of the head. Bobby stood up and gave him a hug.

"You look wonderful yourself, Cityboy," he said. "Life's been good to you." He sat across from Bobby and placed a file on the table between them.

Bobby took in his old friend. In the three decades since he'd last seen him, Bill Densmore had managed to maintain his finely chiseled jawline and physique. Mostly. Unfortunately, he'd lost most of his hair and now sported rimless bifocals.

"And to you as well, counselor," Bobby said. "You look like a lawyer."

Densmore smiled and took a big gulp of the Diet Coke. He gazed at his beautiful wife. "She's easily the best of us," he said. "But our daughter, Eliza, more than anyone else, makes us confident the future is safe from troublemakers. She's in law school up in Denver. I'm sorry you won't get to meet her this trip." He smiled at Bobby. "It's really good to see you, man. What's going on with you?"

Bobby recounted the same condensed version of life after the air force he'd given Fatboy, then filled him in on his trips to North Carolina and San Francisco.

"Allebaugh!" Densmore said. "Can you believe I lived with a gay guy for two years and didn't know it?"

"None of us did," Bobby said. "He's in a good place. Killing it in 'Frisco commercial real estate, and his partner—husband—is a cop. Looks like life's been good to all of us."

"Except for Bensen, of course," Densmore reminded him.

Monika excused herself for a conference call. She would join them for dinner at their club that evening. They sat for a moment, Bobby sipping his St. Pauli Girl. That's a taste you never forget. He pointed to the soft drink.

"Been sober for eleven years," Densmore said. "It got bad for a while. Really bad. Runs in the family, I suppose. I came close to losing Monika and Eliza, so I did a stint in rehab. I stopped drinking, and I focused on them. It's something I should have been doing all along. It took a while, but I finally made peace with all my bad shit since clearing my head."

He hesitated, holding his gaze on Bobby's eyes. "You know, making amends is a big part of getting and keeping sober, Bobby. I'm sorry if I ever was . . . mean-spirited to you about you being Jewish, or from New York, or anything else. I got a lot of nasty programming when I was young, and I've worked diligently to overcome some deeply ingrained prejudices."

Bobby swallowed hard. He was honestly and deeply touched.

"We were kids," Bobby said. "Stupid, immature idiots. But we had a whole lot of fun, right? All of us."

"I never understood what the love of a wonderful woman could do," Densmore said. "Monika means the world to me."

"Easy to see why," Bobby said.

"And she's a monster in court," he said. "You know, she's never lost a case she's litigated."

"I'm not surprised," Bobby said, laughing. "She'd be a hell of a distraction."

"And she'll walk out with your balls tucked neatly inside her Hermès bag."

Densmore's father had cut him out of the family business and any inheritance he might have counted on, but that didn't affect the trust fund Densmore's grandfather, Denny, had put in place. It had been more than sufficient to put both Bill and Monika through college and law school and set them up in Santa Fe where they specialized in real estate, family, and immigration law. Their practice was thriving.

"So, Bensen," Bobby said.

Densmore pushed the file at him. Inside was

Bensen's mug shot. Bobby stared at it, shaking his head. The only recognizable piece of him were his eyes.

"Read," Densmore commanded.

"What is this?"

"It's what I got from Al McCarthy a while back. I didn't look at it again until you reached out."

"I have to call McCarthy and nail down my visit with Bensen in a few days," Bobby said.

"You're going to see him?"

"I have to."

"There's really nothing anyone can do about this. He confessed, and all his appeals ran out." He paused. "Looks like Prettyboy's going to die, Bobby."

"I know. But this is something I have to do. I started down this path and I'm going to finish it."

Bobby scanned the file. It was, he surmised, a condensed version of the case file he'd see at McCarthy's office near Pittsburgh.

Garrett Bensen had confessed to murdering Cletus Tisdale, a Harrisburg police officer, Tisdale's former partner, Arthur Sheffield, and one Joseph "Joey" DiStefano, a street-level creep with convictions for aggravated assault, pimping, and loan sharking.

"So, Bensen confessed he killed a cop, a former cop, and a small-time crook." Bobby read McCarthy's sparse notes about the three additional murder charges Bensen refused to confess to.

"I have a friend who used to be in the Pennsylvania legislature," Densmore said. "Bensen called me when he got arrested, but I'm not licensed to practice there, and I don't do criminal law. I got the name of a referral from my friend and passed it along. I learned the Harrisburg force was notoriously corrupt back then and the local DAs weren't any better. He told me they had several unsolved cases with some really sketchy circumstantial evidence tying them to Bensen, but the prosecutor still tried to clear a few of them on some out-of-towner who happened to be there when the murders occurred. He'd admitted to three killings that took place while he was in Harrisburg. What are three more? They can only execute him once."

None of this was new information. Authors used as many sources of procedural stuff as possible, including cops, lawyers, even bad guys, anyone who could add honesty and texture to a story. The joker in this deck involved the fact that Bensen apparently gave himself up on three of the murders without flinching, but vehemently denied involvement in the other open homicides the HPB and the prosecutor attempted to close with his capture and conviction.

"According to the police file," Densmore said. "He gave them information only the killer would have known involving the crimes, the scene, and specifics of each actual homicide."

By all appearances, Prettyboy took three lives in a place far from home, and far removed from their time together in Germany.

"I'll have access to him next week," Bobby said. "I

don't harbor any illusions about riding in and saving his life at the last minute or anything like that. I write books. Some of them are actually pretty good."

Densmore laughed. "I know. Who'd have thought a kid from Brooklyn who can barely speak American English would become a famous author."

"I don't know about the famous part," Bobby said. "But all our lives took turns none of us expected."

"That's the way it always is," Densmore said. "Sometimes you know someone—but do you really?"

• • •

Dinner at Densmore's club was first rate. Every pair of eyes in the room studied Monika. She'd dressed for the occasion in a form fitting, knee-length black dress, pearls, and a pair of black wedge sandals. Bobby marveled how she fended off advances from men and at least two women. The food was excellent too.

"Can't you do something about this?" Bobby asked Densmore, who threw up his hands in mock surrender.

"Trust me, Cityboy. She can handle herself just fine. Always could."

• • •

May 1983

Two weeks before Bobby left for Turkey, they all were in the Big Dog following a swing shift. Charlotte brought the three Bs to their table—beer, bread, and bratwurst—when a beautiful dark-haired girl walked into the *gasthaus* alone. Densmore sprang to his feet.

"*Eine minute, schatzie,*" Charlotte said, as she dealt their food and beverages onto the table. "Let her get through the door. I'll introduce you."

"I don't want anyone else talking to her," he said. He was staring—gawking— and breathing through his mouth. Bobby was sure Cowboy was close to hyperventilation. He usually played it cool. Not this time.

Charlotte brought her to their table.

"This is Monika Borgen," she said.

"Hi! Bill Densmore," Bill said. He escorted her to a table on the other side of the room. The rest of the crew might as well have been invisible.

Monika Borgen didn't look like the average German girl—big, blue-eyed, and blonde. She was slim with dark brown hair and darker brown eyes. Her face was magnificent. Bobby would later describe her as resembling a young Jacqueline Bissett.

Three months later, at the same time Bobby was struggling to get comfortable in a Quonset hut on a windy hill overlooking the Black Sea near Samsun, Turkey, Densmore surrendered his security clearance and married his way out of a very promising life, including a sizable inheritance and an even more impressive trust fund. He also saved himself from the clutches of the spoiled West Texas woman-child his and her parents had arranged for him to help propel the Densmore dynasty into the future.

The Filthy Five typically fell in love with someone new every week. Maybe even Allebaugh. Cowboy was the first to fall in love for real.

• • •

June 2016

Monika gifted Bobby with another light-up-the-room smile. She returned to the table, sat down, and pecked Densmore on the cheek.

"I knew him when," Bobby said. "I guess he's like fine wine—an acquired taste that improves with age."

"Or maybe cheese," Cowboy said. "Cheese ages well too."

Chapter 6

The next morning, after a brief visit to check out Georgia O'Keefe's best artwork, Bobby drove to Albuquerque and caught a flight that would get him home to Florida—after a stop to change planes in Atlanta. It was an old joke: even if you were going to hell, you'd have to change planes in Atlanta.

The three-hour delay in the world's busiest, most frustrating airport provided an opportunity for Bobby to reconnect with Al McCarthy. He said Bobby could get an hour with Garrett and that Garrett laughed out loud for the first time in years when he heard Bobby's name. Bobby would meet with McCarthy the day before he'd visit Prettyboy.

Deploying his masochistic genes, Bobby Googled "Garrett Bensen" and took another look at the images. Bobby saw his mug shot, a picture from the trial, a couple of boyhood shots, and one of him in uniform. That one. That was the kid he knew. After scrolling down the array of images, he found a current image of

Bensen after two decades on death row. Bobby closed his eyes and shook his head. Prettyboy's hair was gone. He had a goatee and a half-smile that revealed bad teeth. He still looked younger than his years, but the toll of decades on death row was devastating.

Bobby spent a few days in Naples catching Lindy up on what he'd learned on his travels. He knocked out an outline that, up to a point, made sense. He had all the information he needed from their time together in Germany to recreate Bensen's youth and young adulthood. But unless he could spend a lot more time with him before his scheduled execution, Bobby would likely have to resort to speculation, supposition, or outright creation to build a story that worked for readers.

As far as Bobby was concerned, the hook was set. He needed to understand what had happened to this kid. Bobby wanted—needed—insight and whatever might constitute closure. He pitched the story to his editor. She loved it and gave him the green light.

• • •

Born in St. Cloud, Minnesota, Garrett was of Scandinavian, Lutheran heritage. Garrett's father had worked for years in a small furniture factory outside the town of Clearwater until he saved enough money to purchase a gas station and convenience market off I-94, northwest of the Twin Cities.

After Garrett had achieved toddler status, and while

his mother was pregnant with his sister, Ingrid, the family relocated to Eden Prairie, where Garrett participated in an ordinary childhood. This, despite the amount of alcohol his parents consumed. His mother drank all day each day, including when Garrett and his sister, Ingrid, were still buns in the oven. That Garrett and Ingrid weren't impaired by their mother's drinking was testament to the stout and hardy constitution of the individuals themselves. That the elder Bensen's were able to successfully function as both parents and business operators was, according to Garrett, something biologists and sociologists should study.

At Eden Prairie High School, Garrett performed as a steady, if undistinguished, student. He showed little interest in extracurricular activities, didn't plan on college, and demonstrated nothing of an outstanding nature, save for his good looks and charming demeanor. Most days after school he helped his father at the convenience store or tended to household duties while his mother slept off the previous night's bender. He took these responsibilities in stride, doing his best to insulate Ingrid from the harsh realities of his parents' addiction.

His decision to join the air force immediately after escaping from high school surprised his friends and devastated his sister. Ingrid begged him to reconsider, certain she was incapable of replacing him as guardian or support system for their parents'—especially their mother's—sickness. Garrett, still a teenager, was no longer interested in parenting his parents, something he'd done while attempting to have whatever passed for a normal high school experience.

He'd never had to ask a girl for a date; girls flocked to him like ants to a picnic. But the dates weren't satisfying—he was always worried about what he'd find when he got home.

Joining the air force in 1982 was the first selfish thing he'd ever done, and he was good with that decision, until his discharge.

• • •

While Bobby waited for his rental car at Pittsburgh International Airport, he called ahead to see if he could get time with James Warren, the warden at SCI-Greene. An assistant told him the warden would be happy to meet. Bobby decided to save his other requests for their visit, scheduled one hour before he was to see Garrett.

The state correctional institution at Waynesburg housed all forty-seven of Pennsylvania's capital inmates. It was in Greene County and employed lethal injection to dispatch the state's worst offenders.

That lethal injection constituted a more "humane" manner of taking a person's life had always puzzled Bobby. If someone committed murder by injecting a hotshot of heroin into their victim, would leniency apply because the killing was more humane than strangulation, drowning, or bleeding out from a gunshot wound? Bobby believed the words "killing" and "humane" went together about as well as spaghetti and maple syrup.

Bobby arrived a day early and checked himself into a Hampton Inn near the facility. He wondered if everyone he saw had someone scheduled to die under Pennsylvania's allegedly humane method of execution.

After he got settled in his room, Bobby called Johnny Lee. Farmboy told him he admired what Bobby was doing but wouldn't be there watching when Prettyboy took the needle.

"I'm just not strong that way," he said.

"I'm not going to let him die alone," Bobby said.

"When you see him," Farmboy said. "Would you tell him that I love him? And that God forgives him?"

When they were all stationed together, Garrett demonstrated a strong, unwavering faith. Of the five, he and Johnny were the ones who attended services. Garrett was a practicing Lutheran, Johnny, a Southern Baptist.

. . .

Bobby's call to Allebaugh went to voice mail. He dialed Densmore Borgen and was put through to Cowboy.

"You will never guess who's sitting across from me," Densmore said.

"Your beautiful wife?" Bobby asked.

"Nope," he said. "Some gay guy, think we used to call him Fatboy?"

That got a smile out of Bobby. If nothing else good came from this adventure of his, helping reconnect two of his old friends after twenty-some years was sufficient payoff.

"Excellent," Bobby said. "I just tried calling him. Put me on speaker and I can—" Bobby heard the click.

"Three out of five," Allebaugh said. "It appears we have a quorum."

Bobby filled them in about his upcoming meetings and his chat with Farmboy.

"We'll give him a call," Densmore said. "He doesn't get a pass on this. If we're there, then he's damn well going to be there."

"I'll see about getting it cleared with the warden when I meet him," Bobby said, although he was unsure if any of them would get permission to witness the execution of a confessed triple murderer. *Probably not,* Bobby thought, *if Senator Ed Ianucci has anything to say about it.*

"We're going to be there," Allebaugh said. "And I'm bringing a surprise."

"I don't think they like surprises at executions," Bobby said.

"Trust me. They'll be okay with this surprise."

Chapter 7

Senator Ianucci exploded in anger when, during a campaign staff meeting, he learned Garrett Bensen was to have a visitor.

"Who the fuck is this Kaminsky character?" he demanded.

"According to our eyes and ears at Waynesburg, he's an author who knew Bensen back in the early 1980s," Tommy Cavanaugh said. "They were in the air force together."

"I want to know who he is and what he wants with Bensen," Ianucci said. "First thing tomorrow, call the fucking warden and tell him there are no visitors to inmates on the row except for lawyers and immediate family. Is this Kaminsky guy a lawyer or immediate family?"

"I'll make the call," Cavanaugh said. "But I don't think we can stop the warden from—"

"You don't get paid to think!" Ianucci said. "I do the thinking. You just do what the fuck I tell you to do. I want to know everything said and done as soon as this visit is finished. If you have to, go down and meet with this guy yourself. And remind the warden which senator heads the committee that funds his goddamn prison."

Cavanaugh held his tongue in front of the rest of the staff.

"Polling has us neck and neck with Tom Hill. I don't want anything, and I repeat, *anything*, bumping this train off track."

"I'll take care of it, Senator."

• • •

There are people in life who simply do not aspire to lead. Either the spotlight scares them, or they are content to sit behind and whisper into the ear of power. Tommy Cavanaugh was perfectly satisfied to be Ed Ianucci's hands, the get-it-done guy working behind the scenes. In the nooks and crannies of Pennsylvania's state government apparatus, players knew that if they were hearing from Tommy Cavanaugh, they were hearing from the senator. If they wanted to petition Ianucci directly, they went through Cavanaugh.

The two had been close since law school. When Ianucci first went to work as a young prosecutor in Harrisburg, he brought Cavanaugh along to the Dauphin County District Attorney's office. They stayed together when Ianucci ran for the top job in the DA's office. When he announced for the state senate,

Tommy managed his campaign. After Ianucci won, he made Cavanaugh his top aide. Loyalty mattered above all to Ed Ianucci. In Tommy's mind, Ed was destined to be the next governor of Pennsylvania. Someday, Cavanaugh believed, Ed Ianucci would hold even a higher national office.

Tommy knew early on that Ianucci had audacious ambitions, and that the man would do pretty much whatever it took to fulfill them. But the senator didn't care to get his own hands dirty. That's where Tommy came in. Tommy had hitched his career wagon to Ianucci's ambitions. If he had any qualms about his role, he kept them to himself.

. . .

The next morning, Bobby headed to Mt. Lebanon where Al McCarthy, Garrett's lawyer, kept his office. McCarthy was sixty-something, white-haired, and used a wheelchair. Before Bobby could ask, McCarthy told him that thirteen years earlier, when he was a working criminal defense lawyer, a drug addict he'd represented in a nothing street-dealing case had shot him in the back.

"All I do now is handle death row appeals," he said, waving at a wall unit filled with file boxes. "Even though no one has been executed in Pennsylvania for a while now, business on the row, unfortunately, is booming."

"Looks like that streak is about to end," Bobby said. "I must ask. What happened to the guy who shot you?"

"Girl. Seventeen years old, strung out on crystal meth, could barely lift the gun. I think the plan was to off herself, but she misfired. *Et voila.*"

He'd obviously told this tale before. Bobby listened with an author's ears.

"She was out on bail awaiting trial," McCarthy said. "She should have been in a treatment program. I was trying to make that happen. She finished the job on herself three months later while she was in county lockup."

He told Bobby it would be a good idea to review Bensen's case file, as much as would be possible, before meeting with the warden.

"He's easily the most frustrating client I've had," McCarthy explained. "The conviction on the three murders is unbreakable. He had good counsel. Claimed self-defense but based on the lack of any witness to what really happened in that alley, plus the condition of the victims, I don't think anybody bought that. He showed no remorse, and he didn't provide any explanation as to why he killed those three, except that they were scumbags who deserved to die. After his mandated appeals, he said he wouldn't be chasing any more delays or reversals."

"Makes it hard to do your job," Bobby said.

"Yeah," he said. "Like everyone else, I'd just like to

know what the hell happened. He seemed—seems—like a decent guy."

Bobby exhaled a sigh. "We all feel that way."

He told McCarthy about their crew and about their time together in the service. "I'm just glad he agreed to see me," Bobby said.

"I don't think he's had an outside visitor for a dozen years or more," McCarthy said. "Last was his sister, Ingrid. He told her to forget about him and get on with her life."

"So, other than you, he hasn't had any visitors?"

"Jim Warren lets me know when any of my clients in his facility have visitors," he said. "Bensen has no real life to speak of. None of them do. Your guy spends twenty-two hours a day alone in a seven-by-twelve room. Has all his meals there. They never turn off the lights, even when he sleeps. When he exercises, it's in a cage only marginally larger than his cell."

Bobby exhaled and sat at the table with the case file.

"His is the only capital case I've ever litigated where I can't reconcile the deed with the doer."

"The warden an okay guy?" Bobby asked. McCarthy nodded.

"Yeah, he is. Jim Warren has a crappy job," he said. "Most wardens do. People get it in their heads that the warden can change what police, DAs, judges, juries, and guilty defendants are responsible for. But the warden is just a cog in the machinery that fulfills the state's role in dispensing justice."

"How's your relationship with him?"

"It's good. We understand each other and do our best to see that the process goes as smoothly as possible," McCarthy said. "I've had clients who've maintained innocence until time arrives for the sentence to be carried out. Then, they either beg Jesus for forgiveness or wail like old women at an Italian funeral. Others are career bad guys comfortable in a maximum-security prison, even a death-row setting. They tell me to stretch things out as long as I can. Often, something other than the needle does them in"—he made air quotes with his hands—"'natural causes.' There are still a half-dozen guys who've been there longer than Bensen."

He hesitated a moment. Bobby fixed his eyes on the lawyer.

"You know, I make an okay living doing this," McCarthy sighed. "Every now and then, I get a sentence commuted. I would love to see that for Garrett Bensen. About six years ago, I got one overturned. But most of my work is limited to filing motions, follow-up with family, and being there if or when the sentence gets carried out. That hasn't happened in a long time."

"And then we've got Garrett," Bobby said.

McCarthy nodded. "And then we've got Garrett," he repeated. "I know it sounds strange, but you may actually want to talk to Ed Ianucci about Garrett's case."

"And why would I do that? Or really, why would he?"

"I know, I know. It's counterintuitive. But there were

things that bothered me and a few other of Garrett's lawyers about the way his prosecution played out."

"You mean the thing about Garrett admitting to the three but denying the others?"

"Yes," McCarthy said. "Not a single witness surfaced who had any knowledge of the crimes. There was no weapon or any real forensic evidence. Just Garrett's guilty plea to offing these creeps—Tisdale, Sheffield, and DiStefano."

"I've always understood the prosecution needs to prove three elements in order to get a conviction—means, motive, and opportunity," Bobby said. "Did Garrett or Ianucci ever provide a reason as to why someone with a clean record, who wasn't from Harrisburg, would come from out of town just to kill three people, two of them cops?"

"Not that I know of." McCarthy wheeled himself over to the file boxes, rummaged through them, and pulled out a file. He flipped pages until he found what he was looking for.

"This is Garrett's first interview," he said. "Taken after he was brought to Harrisburg, but before he was officially charged. Here," he said, pointing. Bobby took the file and read it out loud.

Ianucci: "Did you know Cletus Tisdale, Arthur Sheffield, and Joseph DiStefano?"

Bensen: "Well enough to know that they were pieces of human waste who deserved to be flushed, once and for all."

Bobby looked at McCarthy. "I guess he really didn't like these three gentlemen."

"Keep reading."

He read the next two pages before stopping and looking quizzically at McCarthy.

"Ianucci never followed up, never asked why Garrett felt that way, never dug any deeper," McCarthy said. "He was happy with that one sentence, which by itself constituted a remorseless confession."

Bobby asked about the other three victims, two of whom were criminals, but McCarthy told him that Garrett repeatedly and vehemently denied knowing any of them or killing anyone other than Tisdale, Sheffield, and DiStefano.

"Is Garrett's trial attorney available?" he asked.

"No. Unfortunately, Jack Parks died three years ago," McCarthy said. "He was a good defense attorney, but Garrett didn't give him a lot to work with."

Bobby wrote crime fiction, so he'd read police files, court transcripts, depositions, and witness statements. Nowhere in any of the cases he'd researched did he ever encounter a death sentence without testimony from witnesses, evidence from crime scene forensics, from anything other than a stoic confession. There's a lot of precedent for cases being pleaded down when the defendant is guilty, confesses, and expresses remorse. But it didn't happen in Garrett's case. He pleaded not guilty and demonstrated absolutely no remorse.

Bobby asked McCarthy why he thought Ed Ianucci would consent to talk to him. McCarthy smiled.

"Ed Ianucci is a political animal," he said. "He thinks he's the smartest guy in the room. I don't really know if he'll consent to visit with you, but his ego, which is the size of Pittsburgh, probably won't let him lose the opportunity to convince you your friend needs to die."

"I'll think about it," Bobby said.

"I'm surprised Benson actually wants to see you," McCarthy said. "I sent a summary of this file to another friend years ago, but nothing came of it. When I mentioned your name, he actually laughed. 'I would absolutely love to see Cityboy Bobby Kaminski.' His exact words."

Bobby asked McCarthy if he thought the four of them would be able to witness Bensen's execution. He placed the odds of that at about 30 percent.

"What about the other three cases they tried to hang on Garrett?"

McCarthy exhaled and shook his head.

"The Harrisburg system was a hot, stinking mess at that time," he said. "Personally, I think Ianucci wanted to feather his own nest by making Bensen into more of a bad guy than he already was."

"What finally happened?"

"The trial judge, who ultimately was removed from the bench for soliciting and accepting bribes, threw out the charges on the other three," he said. "There are probably news accounts of how that went down but

I can't help but believe Senator Ianucci is still pissed he couldn't get those cases cleared."

Bobby thanked McCarthy for his time. He made a mental note to investigate those other cases. He pondered the notion of going to see Senator Ianucci. That would necessitate a trip to Harrisburg. He drove the hour back to Waynesburg, went to his room at the Hampton Inn, and transcribed his notes.

Chapter 8

The next morning at SCI-Greene Penitentiary, Bobby and his escort were buzzed through six different sets of locked doors, up one staircase and down another, before arriving at the warden's office. He was made to surrender his phone, wallet, and keys, and was professionally frisked. After that gauntlet, he entered a spacious, well-lit room featuring a polished wooden writing table, an ergonomic executive chair, a bookcase showcasing resin busts of Voltaire and Tolstoy, and a view overlooking the low-slung barracks of Pennsylvania's maximum-security state prison. He laughed when he saw a copy of his last book, *Murder in the Fifth*, on top of the table.

"Yes, Mr. Kaminsky, I'm a fan of your work," Jim Warren said, extending a hand. The warden of Pennsylvania's maximum-security prison stood nearly six and a half feet tall, was thin as a sapling, and hunched over from a nasty case of scoliosis. If he'd had a few more pounds on his body, the warden could have played *Richard III.*

"Can I inscribe that for you?"

"That's why it's out," he said, handing over a fountain pen.

Bobby wrote him a personal note and signed his name, leaving the book open to let the ink dry before it went back on the shelf.

"I should tell you: Garrett Bensen hasn't seen anyone from the outside world in a very long time, except for Al McCarthy, and even that has been a couple years," the warden said. "It's puzzling, but nice that he's going to sit with you." He said they'd have about an hour, maybe an hour and a half with the prisoner.

"I want to see how it goes for each of you before committing any further," he said. "I know you're an author and might see a book in his case. If everyone's okay after today, you can visit again. We'll evaluate after each visit."

Bobby asked him about Prettyboy's prison experience. Not surprising—Garrett was a model inmate, so much so that he'd been granted privileges other death-row residents typically didn't earn.

"You have to understand," Warren said, "Garrett killed a cop and an ex-cop. Out in the world, he may be a pariah, but in here—especially since they turned out to be bad cops—he's a celebrity. Sometimes he'll ask for a legal pad and pencils," he said. "Obviously, we don't give writing implements to people who could use them in a manner that might shorten their time here. That's not the case with Garrett."

He paused. Bobby chose to not interrupt the warden's information dump.

"It's hard for me to reconcile the person I've come to know and the person who confessed to those murders," he said. "Garrett is thoughtful, polite—quite disarming, if you know what I mean."

"Oh, I absolutely know," Bobby said. "We lived together for a year. We were as close as two kids could be. Relationships in the military are like shipboard romances—without the romance part. One night, Garrett and I damn near died together. That kind of experience matters in a relationship, at any age."

• • •

August 1982

Garrett and Bobby truly bonded after Bobby flipped Gerry Archworth's VW Beetle on the road from Frankfurt to Darmstadt.

They'd enjoyed a typically useless visit to the big city chasing *frauleins* and guzzling beer in a variety of bars, all within walking distance of the Frankfurt train station. Why they hadn't taken the train became a consistent and annoying topic of conversation after the accident. At the time, Bensen didn't even have a driver's license and Bobby only had his for a year.

Whenever they could, they borrowed wheels instead of indenturing themselves to train schedules.

On the drive from Frankfurt, they discussed the opportunities they'd squandered with a couple of attractive older women, older meaning nearly thirty. They were both in for an all-nighter but didn't have a place to crash and neither Bobby nor Garrett had cash for hotel rooms.

The car they drove was useless for any kind of party. It was a stripped down 1975 VW Beetle with a load capacity of two people, period. Archworth, the VW's owner, was a big, strapping farm kid from upstate New York. How he folded himself into such a small space was anyone's guess.

After much frustration, lamentation, and negotiation, they promised to meet Ulla and Christa the following weekend, after payday, and began their trip back to Darmstadt.

Halfway into the trip, they came upon a ninety-degree right turn, which they took way too fast. They were gabbing and laughing when the turn materialized. Bobby was driving. No seat belts. Drunk.

They were probably going thirty-five kph when the turn started. The car had no center of gravity. It went up on two wheels, flipped onto the passenger's side, then onto the roof, then onto the driver's side, coming to rest on the steps of a police station. It was the middle of the night and made quite a racket.

"*Vas ist los?*" the police officer asked, as he and his

colleague came out of the police station. *What's wrong?* Bensen was laughing, a good sign, but inappropriate to the occasion. Bobby reached across, rolled down the window and waved.

"I'm okay," he said. "We're okay."

Tall and lean at the time, Bobby wriggled himself across Garrett's body and through the open window. Garrett continued enjoying some private joke. The police officers walked around the car twice, looked at one another, and then motioned Bobby to join them. The car was on its side; Garrett was half in his seat, and half in Bobby's, with his left arm pressed against the window on the driver's side. Bobby and the two cops slipped their hands under the roofline and lifted the car and Garrett. To Bobby's surprise, the car landed on its wheels with a single, stabilizing bounce. Garrett got his bearings, looked out the window, smiled, and provided an exaggerated thumbs-up. Both doors were fused shut by the accident.

Bobby thanked the officers. They bid the two a "*guten morgen*" and told them to have a safe trip back to their post.

"Do you think the car will drive?" Bobby asked. The officers looked at each other. Both shrugged their shoulders.

"It's German," one said, with pride. "Of course, it will."

Bobby climbed through the driver-side window and into the seat he'd occupied before the VW achieved its triple flip. The keys were in the ignition, right where he'd left them. He cranked it up, and the motor turned right over. Bobby pushed in the clutch, put the VW in gear, and they headed down the road. It was like nothing had even happened—except for the caved in roof and the fused-shut doors.

"What are we going to tell Archworth?" Garrett asked.

"He's on leave for another eight days or so," Bobby said. "Let's see what we can come up with before he gets back."

Gerry Archworth had bought the used VW from a departing army guy for nine hundred dollars six months earlier. He didn't put a dime into it, just bought it and drove it. These old VW Beetles could take a lot of punishment.

Bensen had about four hundred dollars saved. Bobby had another three hundred, plus he could tap Densmore for some loose change if necessary. Guys in the motor pool told Bobby it could cost as much as eight hundred, depending on what Archworth wanted to do. It would deplete both their savings accounts but, in the end, they'd do what they had to do.

Bensen and Bobby were in their room when Archworth stopped by. He was big and broad, like a defensive tackle. Bobby wondered to himself, how in the hell did Archworth even fit into that car?

"You idiots okay?" he asked.

"Yeah," Bobby started. "Look, I'm—"

"You gonna make this right?"

"Absolutely."

"Of course," Bensen added.

"Let's go outside," Archworth said.

They ran down the staircase and out the front door of their barracks building into the dirt lot where guys parked their cars. The VW was in the front row, facing the barracks. Archworth used both hands to yank the passenger door open, reached his right arm inside, and pushed the roof back where it was supposed to be.

"Damn," Bensen said, admiringly.

"Another inch and one of you idiots might have been dead," Archworth said. "Whoever was driving—"

"That would be me," Bobby said.

Archworth got in, started the bug, and drove it around the parking lot testing all three speeds. Then he parked, opened the rear hood, and checked the back. Bobby thought the VW's engine looked like something you'd find in a lawn mower.

Archworth went around to the driver's door, yanked it open, slammed it back shut, and pulled it open again. He did the same one more time to the passenger side door.

"Looks like everything works," he said. "And it's fucking amazing none of the glass shattered. What happened?"

They told him everything, including how the German police put the car back on its wheels.

"And you jerkoffs are both okay?" Archworth asked. "No issues?"

They were golden.

"I'll be in touch," he said.

They never heard from him about what they owed him for messing up his ride. From then on, whenever they were in town and he was there, either Bobby or Garrett always picked up the tab when they were together, which was no small potatoes for a man so large.

• • •

July 2016

That near-death experience superglued their relationship, though Bensen just saw it as a wasted road trip to Frankfurt. When Bensen turned eighteen, he finally got his driver's license, compliments of the United States air force.

• • •

Bobby and Jim Warren shared a few other Garrett stories. Then, the warden checked the time and called for an escort.

"I'm sorry about the formalities, but we need to do this a specific way."

They walked past a row of steel doors configured with small slits that allowed the guards to see inside. They turned a corner and came to a door marked *Interview*.

A corrections officer opened it. A second officer

went and declared the room clear and available. The warden pointed to a chair.

"If you would, please sit on the near side of the table. Garrett will come through that far door and will be chained to the desk and chair. The Plexiglas is visitation protocol for inmates on death row."

A sheet of thick plastic extended across the whole of the room, with a hole about six inches in diameter covered by a tight-fitting metal screen in the middle. Visitors and inmates could talk but nothing would pass between them. There would be no physical contact of any kind.

"Can I at least shake hands with him?" Bobby asked.

"Sorry, but I'm afraid not. It'll be just a few moments."

Bobby was surprised at how anxious he felt.

The back door to the room opened and a guard entered. Jim Warren came next, followed by Garrett and another guard.

"Please remain seated," one of the guards said. His nametag read *Fouser.*

Garrett smiled broadly at Bobby.

"Bobby K. from Sheepshead Bay," he said. "What's a nice Jewish boy from Brooklyn doing in a high-class joint like this?"

Bobby filed away the snappy retort that jumped into his mouth.

"Visiting an old friend," he said. "God, man, you look like shit."

"We'll leave you two sweethearts alone," said

Warden Warren. "It's 11:25 a.m." A guard recorded the time. "We'll be back at one unless things get out of hand. Remember, we can see and hear everything, so no speaking in a foreign language and no ballroom dancing."

Bensen thanked the warden and the guards, all by name. Bobby just nodded to signal his understanding of the rules and his appreciation. The room went silent. Then Garrett laughed.

"It took you long enough. How'd you find out?" he asked.

"Saw a piece in *USA Today* about your impending appointment with the reaper," Bobby said. "It's been old-home week ever since." Bobby caught him up on Fatboy, Cowboy, and Farmboy.

"God, I've thought so much about that time," he said. "I've had a lot of time to think since they put me in here. That was the best time of my life."

When they were in Germany, Garrett weighed maybe one sixty-five on a lean five-foot, ten-inch frame. At the time, he had black hair, his Swedish father's bright blue eyes, and white, white teeth. This person across from Bobby scaled 25 percent heavier. His eyes had faded to a soft blue-gray, and his teeth were awful, yellow, and stained. He looked old, tired, defeated.

"I know a few things," Bobby said. "I know I'm the first person you've agreed to see in a really long time." Prettyboy nodded his head. "And I really appreciate you letting me visit. I know you confessed to three murders, which I cannot get my head around, and I know you've never talked about motives or reasons." Benson stared at his old roomie before looking down and then away.

"Before you leave today, Bobby, there's some stuff I'd like you to have," Benson said. "Maybe after you go through it, we can talk at length about it." He looked at Bobby with intensity and rapped his knuckles against the table. "You're the only one I'll share any of this with."

Bobby promised he would take good care of whatever Garrett gave him. He studied his old roommate, trying to see a murderer. There were differences, of course, the wear and tear of two decades on death row.

"I'm thinking of writing a book," Bobby said. "Would you mind?"

There wasn't a moment's hesitation. He nodded.

"Oh yeah, absolutely, yeah," he said. "Once they're done with me you can do whatever you want. Whatever you think is right."

They reminisced about trips to Amsterdam, the time they all went to Bremerhaven to pick up Densmore's gold Chevy. They called it the Golden Buzzard. They laughed about Johnny's conquests, Bobby's books, which Garrett told him he'd read and reread, and the pinochle games Prettyboy always managed to lose. Each of these triggered other memories, which took them to other places and introduced other characters.

The only thing missing from the visit was a sixer of St. Pauli Girl.

Garrett told Bobby he knew Allebaugh was gay before anyone else.

"After you rotated, I stumbled into a place in Frankfurt and saw him there. I left when I realized where I was. I don't think he saw me. I didn't see any reason to bring it up."

"Actually," Bobby said, smiling. "He did see you that night. He wanted to know if you enjoyed your dance with, what was her name . . . Emerald?" Garrett laughed at the memory.

"Drunk as I was," Garrett said, "I was not up for that! Got me sober in a hurry."

"Apparently, Emerald was 'up' for a dance with you, my boy."

Garrett gave that a smile and a nod.

"Well," Bobby said, "Fatboy sends his love. So does Farmboy, and so does Cowboy."

"The Filthy Five," Prettyboy said. "What a bunch of knuckleheads we were."

"We had fun," Bobby said. "What the fuck happened, Garrett?"

Garrett's face changed, just a little. Bobby tried to grab onto what he was seeing. Anger? Sadness? Regret?

"Everything that happened, it all goes back to Darmstadt."

Bobby told him he didn't follow.

"I need you to read something," Benson said. "Come back tomorrow, or in a few days if you can. Okay, Bobby?"

Bobby wanted to unpack what Garrett was saying, but he didn't want to upset him.

"I will, I promise."

He looked up at a camera and nodded his head, holding up a peace sign. Two minutes.

"Do you remember Kathy Cobb?" Garrett asked out of nowhere.

Bobby searched his memory for a minute.

"I remember Major Cobb," he said. Major Frederick Douglass Cobb had been their unit commander. He couldn't enter the compound where they'd performed their intelligence duties because he had, earlier in his career, married a German woman and consequently lost his top-secret security clearance. That had all happened years earlier, when then–First Lieutenant Cobb was stationed in Wiesbaden, just after the end of things in Vietnam. It was the same thing with Densmore when he married Monika. Marry a foreign national; say goodbye to your security clearance.

"The major's daughter!" Bobby finally said, recalling a beautiful light-skinned Black girl. Bensen smiled.

"Do some research," he said. The door opened and the guards came in. They unshackled Garrett and escorted him out.

Chapter 9

A guard met Bobby outside the interview room and guided him into the anteroom outside Jim Warren's office. The warden passed by Bobby and said, "Let's talk. Have a seat."

The warden handed over a stack of yellow legal pads filled with neat script.

"You're the only person other than me who's seen this," he said. "And I'm not sure I've seen all of it. Maybe it'll shed some light on the cloudy areas. Maybe you'll be able to add context."

He put the yellow legal pads into a large manila envelope.

Bobby's heart raced. He was hungry to devour whatever it was Garrett had written. He thanked Jim Warren, picked up his personal effects, and was escorted out of the penitentiary. It was a stormy afternoon in Waynesburg, Pennsylvania.

When he got behind the wheel of his rental car, his phone rang. He didn't recognize the number.

"Hello?"

"Is this Robert Kaminsky?"

"It is. Who's asking?" Bobby asked.

"My name is Eduard Ianucci," the voice said. "Senator Eduard Ianucci."

"Okay," Bobby said.

"I understand you visited Garrett Bensen at SCI-Greene today," he said.

"You understand correctly, Senator."

"What was the purpose of your visit, Mr. Kaminski?"

That was all it took. Bobby immediately disliked Senator Eduard Ianucci. He wanted to ask why the hell that was any of his fucking business. Instead, he chose to be polite, sort of.

"What is the purpose of your inquiry, Senator?"

"Listen, Kaminski," he said, dropping any pretense of collegiality. "I don't know who you are or what you think you're doing down there, but Garrett Bensen killed six people in Harrisburg twenty-seven years ago. I know this because I'm the guy who prosecuted him. He was guilty, he confessed, he was convicted by a jury, and he's going to die."

"Thank you for the history lesson, Senator, but I already knew all of that," Bobby said. "Except . . . Wasn't the number three, and not six?"

"It was six. A timid judge made an awful decision about the others."

"The number doesn't really matter, though, right,

Senator?" Bobby asked. "He's still scheduled to take the needle, isn't he?"

"That's right. So, what's the purpose of you visiting him?" Ianucci asked. "He hasn't had visitors in years outside of his lawyer." Bobby shook his head. So much for politeness.

"My purpose for visiting him is none of your damn business." There was a pause on the line.

"Do yourself a favor, Mr. Kaminsky. Go back home and leave Garrett Bensen to the Commonwealth of Pennsylvania."

"How about I come to Harrisburg instead?" Bobby mused. "And you and I spend some time talking about the oddities in Bensen's case."

Ianucci snorted. "What are you, writing a book?"

Bobby laughed. "In fact, I am. It'll be my seventh. What are you doing? Running for governor?"

"Just make damn sure you stay out of the people's business, Mr. Kaminski. My reach is long."

That sounded an awful lot like a threat. Bobby hesitated. How did he know Bobby had visited Garrett? How did he know Bobby's number? And how did he happen to know all of it so quickly? When some asshole pissed him off, Bobby K. from Sheepshead Bay let his inner street kid push his way up to the surface.

"If your reach is so long, why don't you just go fuck yourself?" Bobby ended the call before Ianucci could respond. "Asshole."

• • •

Most of what Garrett had given him would provide excellent background for the book. He wrote in detail about growing up in Minnesota, his messy family life, and his school experiences before joining the air force. He provided insights into relationships Bobby would tap into when the time came. He wrote his impressions and memories about the group excursions the Five had together. There was quotable content, enough for a book, and there was material that would likely never see the light of day.

A stunning revelation involved Kathy Cobb, the major's daughter. Bobby only vaguely recalled the girl. He'd seen her a time or two in the Airman's Club, but that was about it. Garrett, on the other hand, spent time with her while they both took college courses through the University of Maryland. When Bobby left for Turkey, Garrett had twenty-four months left on his enlistment. According to his notes, his plan was to get his degree, apply for Officer Candidate School, marry Kathy, and make a career in the air force. On these handwritten pages, and strictly from his own point of view, Garrett Bensen and Kathy Cobb were in love.

Bobby went through all six yellow pads. He found nothing that contributed to an understanding of motive for Garrett committing the three murders for which he'd confessed and was convicted.

He read through a passage involving a second brawl,

later in his enlistment. Garrett apparently had been walking back to barracks after meeting Kathy when two guys jumped him. They pounded him about the face and body, called him a nigger-loving punk, and left him bleeding about a hundred yards from the barracks. This second beating felt a great deal like the one earlier in his tour, but he wrote he had no idea who "the two rednecks" were.

• • •

Cityboy reached out to Cowboy, Fatboy, and Farmboy. Prettyboy was the last of them to be assigned to Germany, and he'd still been there after they'd moved on, leaving him without their support. None of them knew about this second beating. Johnny was the only one who had known about Garrett and Kathy Cobb but, according to Garrett's narrative, never thought or said anything about it.

At this point, Garrett was in this all by himself.

Bobby felt a pang of remorse for taking reassignment. Had he finished his entire three-year tour in Darmstadt he'd have been around to help Garrett. The gang might have held together a little while longer.

The fifteen months Bobby spent in Samsun, Turkey, had cleansed much of his memory. He recalled little from his time in Turkey, so it was no surprise he also lost most of the good times from Germany. *This might have been different*, he thought, *but it was what it was.*

He would base any future steps on realities, and not on the wouldas, the couldas, and the shouldas.

• • •

Garrett never graduated from the University of Maryland, or from any other college for that matter. Before his enlistment ended, Kathy and her family rotated back to the States when Major Cobb was promoted to lieutenant colonel. He was assigned to a cooling-out post at Electronic Security Command, Wright Patterson Air Force Base in Dayton, Ohio. Garrett and Kathy continued to correspond even after Lt. Colonel Cobb retired.

Prettyboy had written about returning to Minneapolis after being discharged, only to learn his parents had split. His mother was in the wind and his father was still a nasty drunk. Garrett found work in St. Paul as a Teletype operator for an airline and lived with his sister, Ingrid, and her boyfriend, Keith, who worked as a major appliance repairman. He kept in touch with Kathy but didn't see her again until after her father had retired and they'd moved home to Pittsburgh.

This was the first clue as to why Garrett ended up in Pennsylvania, and to Harrisburg as well. Pittsburgh is two hundred miles west of Harrisburg, about three and a half hours on I-70.

• • •

Bobby took a break and headed to a nearby Outback Steakhouse for dinner. While waiting for his order, he ruminated on something he had learned from Garrett's writings. Two beatings, eighteen months apart, a controversial relationship, but it was still a while before the murders, and still more before he was finally caught, arrested, and prosecuted.

After finishing his dinner, a short, well-dressed man greeted him in the parking lot.

"Mr. Kaminski?"

Bobby recalled his earlier conversation with Ed Ianucci, but this guy didn't appear at all threatening. Cityboy stopped and just stared at him.

"My name is Tom Cavanaugh. Do you have a moment to talk to me?"

"Do we know each other?"

"No, sir, we don't," he said. "Can I buy you a drink? Or maybe a cup of coffee? I just need a few moments of your time. It's about Garrett Bensen."

"Of course it is," Bobby said. His curiosity was piqued.

They went inside and took seats at the bar. They both ordered coffee.

"So," Bobby asked, "Who are you and what's your interest in my visit with Garrett Bensen?"

"No foreplay. Okay. Fine. Again, my name is Tom Cavanaugh. I'm on staff to state Senator Ed Ianucci. You have, I believe, already been made aware that, as Dauphin County prosecutor, Senator Ianucci obtained a conviction against Garrett Bensen for the murders of three people, including one active-duty police officer, in the city of Harrisburg."

Bobby held himself in check. Why was Ianucci so worked up over a visit by an old friend to a death-row inmate? First, he calls and plays bully. Now, one of his people shows up in the parking lot in front of an Outback Steakhouse near Waynesburg, Pennsylvania. At least this guy wasn't threatening him. What rocks was Bobby turning over? And what was slithering out from underneath them?

"I am aware of that, Mr. Cavanaugh," Bobby said. "I spoke to your boss earlier, right after I left the penitentiary. By the way, how does he know who I am? And how does he know I was visiting my friend? And how did he obtain my mobile phone number? And why is he so wound up over a guy visiting a friend before one of them gets put to sleep?"

Cavanaugh had a habit of resting his hand in front of his mouth; it was a gesture Bobby had learned about from watching his mother, sometimes indicating she had something to say but was holding back.

"Senator Ianucci is a great and powerful man," he began.

Bobby laughed. "Like the great and powerful Oz?" He took a sip of coffee. "He's a state senator, right?"

"Look, I'm sorry, Mr. Kaminski. I mean no disrespect. I'm here simply to ask you what your intentions are regarding Garrett Bensen."

The back of Bobby's neck heated up. He couldn't put his finger on why these seemingly benign questions were getting him so angry. But they were.

"My intentions? Listen, Mr. Cavanaugh, Garrett Bensen is an old and very dear friend of mine who is about to be put to death by the Commonwealth of Pennsylvania. I know he's confessed to three murders, and I fully expect he's going to die in September. My *intentions* are to visit him as much as I can. I've authored a few books. I might write one about Garrett's case. Please pass that along to your great and powerful senator. And please let him know that I am not impressed with his title or his empty threats. Now, if you would, please answer my questions. How does Senator Ianucci know who I am and how did he know I'd visited Garrett today? How did he get my mobile number? Is this how elected officials do business in Pennsylvania?"

Cavanaugh didn't flinch.

"What you need to understand, Mr. Kaminsky, is that he *does* know who you are. He *does* know you visited Garrett Bensen. He *does* know your mobile number. And he *does* know a great deal more than that about you. You'd be well advised to tread lightly, sir."

Bobby threw a ten-dollar bill on the bar. He knew if he didn't leave at that very moment, he might have ended up breaking Tom Cavanaugh's pointy little nose.

Bobby tried to shake off the ham-handed attempts to scare him. Next to his rental Kia, a black SUV had him hemmed in so he couldn't open the driver's door.

Bobby sensed someone step close behind him. As soon as he turned, a solid right hand smashed into the side of his head and a hard knee was delivered to his groin. He dropped to his knees. A second assailant lifted and held him while the first used his fists to pummel Bobby's center, someone trying to send an unambiguous message without leaving marks.

Neither of his assailants said a word. They did their business, got into the Honda Pilot, and drove away.

. . .

When the cobwebs cleared, Bobby punched 911 on his phone but hung up before making contact. When the operator quickly called back, Bobby called them off.

"I'm sorry, I thought for a minute my car had been stolen but then I remembered I had parked it somewhere other than where I was looking," he said.

"You're sure everything is okay, sir?"

"Absolutely," Bobby said. "Thanks. And I'm sorry for any inconvenience."

"You have a good night, sir."

In pain, but able to drive, Bobby returned to his room, downed four Advil, and climbed into the bathtub. He filled it with water as cold as he could stand it.

He decided for the moment to keep quiet about the incident. His face was unmarked. Most of the damage was to his body. He didn't bleed when he peed, had no swelling. No one should have cause to wonder what happened to him.

But Bobby didn't kid himself—this was no ordinary beating. He'd been rude and disrespectful to Senator

Ed Ianucci on the phone and to his lackey, Cavanaugh, in person. This was a planned, professional intervention. Bobby had upset some important people with significant resources who clearly had something to hide.

Chapter 10

Before Bobby went to bed, he noticed a message on his mobile from Jim Warren. He called the warden's number.

"I see you've managed to make friends quickly here in the Keystone State, Mr. Kaminski," he said.

"Ianucci? How'd he know I was there?"

"An excellent question," Warren said. "To which I currently have no answer. The senator is experiencing some severe indigestion regarding your visit with Garrett today. He graced me with a personal call in which he suggested, somewhat aggressively, that I not let you come back."

"I hope I didn't do anything to cause you grief," Bobby said. He kept his encounter with Tom Cavanaugh and the two goons to himself.

"If he somehow he gets elected," Warren sad. "I might have to retire sooner than I want to."

"I'm really sorry, Warden."

Jim Warren paused for a moment, but only a moment. "So, when would you like to come back?"

Bobby stifled a laugh.

"Whenever it's good for Garrett," he said. "And for you, of course. I have some additional information but there are some major gaps and so many questions. And frankly, I'm puzzled about Ianucci's over-the-top interference. Any chance I can stay a little longer if things go okay?"

"I can't see any reason why not," he said. "Come in tomorrow afternoon at 2:00 p.m. If it's okay with Garrett, you can stay until his evening meal at 6:30."

Bobby thanked him. He appreciated the warden going out on a limb for someone he'd just met.

"Don't worry about it," the warden said. "I don't believe Ianucci will be elected governor." He hesitated. "Of course, he got elected to the state senate, so anything is possible."

• • •

The big questions about Garrett's case remained. What precipitated the murders of Tisdale, Sheffield, and DiStefano? What's the story with Kathy Cobb? How did Garrett get caught? What about those other cases Ianucci bundled into Garrett's prosecution? And why didn't Garrett put up a more aggressive defense?

Bobby wondered about Garrett's state of mind now, whether he was truly at peace with his fate.

The next morning, Jim Warren called and asked Bobby to come in an hour earlier. Their visit would be monitored. On his way to the penitentiary, Bobby stopped at a Radio Shack and purchased a small recorder, a dozen microcassette tapes, and two sleeves of AAA batteries.

While he waited, Bobby googled Kathy Cobb, where he stumbled on a link referencing a Kathy Cobb-Bensen. Wide-eyed, he leaned in and clicked. On *The Harrisburg Patriot-News* website was a picture of a beautiful young Black woman under the headline, "Pregnant Woman Bludgeoned to Death in Downtown Harrisburg." Cobb-Bensen? Pregnant? Bludgeoned? He went numb.

"Fuck," he said to himself. The story was dated May 18, 1988. The byline on the story was a reporter named Micah Previn.

> Police discovered the body of a young woman. identified as Kathy Cobb-Bensen, late Tuesday night in an alley behind Calvino's Restaurant in downtown Harrisburg. Dauphin County Medical Examiner Bertram Rickoff said the preliminary cause of death was repeated blunt force trauma to the head and body.

Police sources told The Patriot-News they had no eyewitnesses to the murder. The victim's husband, Garrett Bensen, was himself a victim of a violent mugging earlier in the evening. He was notified of his wife's death while reporting the mugging at Penbrook Police Department on 28th Street.

"According to Mr. Bensen," said HPB Inspector Jeff Costa, "the couple was out for dinner and was walking to their car when he was hit from behind and knocked unconscious."

Bensen said at the time of his questioning he didn't know what had happened to his wife. "When I regained consciousness, she was gone and I had no idea where I was," he said. He also told Inspector Costa he had no idea why he and his wife were targeted.

A patrolling Penbrook Police cruiser spotted Mr. Bensen walking erratically on S. Progress Avenue around 9:00 p.m. Tuesday night. Officer Miles Jacobus brought him to Penbrook PD after he reported being knocked unconscious earlier that evening somewhere in downtown Harrisburg.

"He told me he'd been out for dinner with his wife," Officer Jacobus said. "He said the attack occurred while they were returning to their car."

Police are speculating the crime may have had racial overtones. Mr. Bensen is white. Mrs. Bensen was black. Inspector Costa indicated that although Mrs. Bensen's body was found behind Calvino's Restaurant, the crime did not appear to have occurred there.

"Preliminary evidence indicates Mrs. Bensen's body was dumped in the alley behind Calvino's," Inspector Costa said. He also indicated Mr. Bensen may have been dumped in Penbrook.

Mr. Bensen told police he wasn't sure exactly where they were when he was attacked, which, Costas said, occurred several hours before Medical Examiner Rickoff's estimated time of death for Mrs. Bensen at 10:30 p.m. Tuesday night.

Penbrook PD confirmed Mr. Bensen was brought into their 28th Street facility at 9:15 p.m. He was taken to UPMC Pinnacle Osteopathic at 11:15 p.m. for treatment of his wounds.

An HPB patrol unit discovered Mrs. Bensen's body just after midnight while investigating a barking dog complaint behind Calvino's Restaurant.

Kathy Cobb-Bensen was 25 years old.

The HPB requests any information that could assist in solving both Mrs. Bensen's murder and Mr. Bensen's mugging be reported to an anonymous tip line at 1-800-333-HPB5.

Bobby's head fell back onto the top of his chair. He stared at the ceiling. Garrett and Kathy were married. They were expecting their first child. He was mugged, she was abducted, beaten, murdered, and her body was dumped. He shut his laptop and headed to SCI-Greene to see Garrett.

• • •

Garrett was already in place in the interview room when Bobby arrived. He smiled when Bobby walked in.

"That's the look of a man who's learned some things," he said.

"I don't know what to say," Bobby said. "I mean, where do I even start?"

Garrett leaned in and spoke for the recording device. "Even when I was arrested, which was years after I killed those assholes, the HPB was still a corrupt, racist cesspool. There was no one to go to for anything resembling justice. When they murdered Kathy and nearly killed me, it was just business as usual for these scumbags."

Bobby was filled with questions. It took him a moment to organize his thoughts.

"When did you figure out cops were involved?"

Garrett smiled and shook his head. "Just before I got clubbed, I remember we were cutting through an unlit side street. I heard someone say, 'Gonna be a rough night for you, Bubba.'" Garrett paused. "*Bubba.* It was partly the voice, but what struck me was the whole 'Bubba' thing. You remember that beating down the road from the *gasthaus* in Darmstadt? One of those assholes also called me 'Bubba' that night. Told me I should watch who I talk to in town and that Charlotte—that waitress at the Dog—was off-limits. Then one of them held me while the other one worked me over.

"Same two assholes kicked the shit out of me again the night Kathy and I left the Airman's Club. That happened after you left for Turkey. The same guy 'Bubba-ed' me that night. I recognized his voice. Told me, 'Where I come from, Bubba, chocolate and vanilla don't mix.' At least he left her alone that night."

"You suspected they might be the same guys, but you didn't know who they were. Is that right?" Bobby asked.

"Not at the time," he said. "I wasn't sure about them being cops, either, until later."

Bobby said they would cover that later. For now, he wanted to know about the years Garrett had with Kathy before she was murdered.

"I worked fixing appliances with my brother-in-law up in Minneapolis," he said. "Once I figured out what I was doing, I realized I could do that kind of work anywhere, and I wanted to be near her. I moved to Pittsburgh in 1987 and then, after we got married, we moved to Harrisburg. That was in September '88."

"What a coincidence, to end up in the same place as these guys?" Bobby asked.

Garrett nodded. "Yeah, it was. I had told myself that someday I would find those assholes and make them pay for what they did to me," he said. "But that was just the angry, young kid in me talking. I had no idea they would be living not too far from where we were."

"But you and Kathy had good years, right?"

"Every day was good, but it wasn't enough. Before they did what they did to us, and to . . ." He swallowed hard, obviously remembering his unborn child. "Like I said, I knew I was going to find some way to get back at them. Then they went and did what they did."

"How'd the two of you meet?" Bobby asked. "It wasn't like the CO's daughter was part of our social circle."

Garrett laughed. "Social circle? Is that what we were?" That was one description of the Filthy Five.

"It was like *South Pacific*," Garrett said. "After you left for Turkey and the Five became Four, we didn't really do all that much. I hung out at the Airman's Club. Between the WAFs, the local girls with ID cards, and the civilians working on the post, there were plenty of available girls . . . women, I guess. Then, one night, I saw her on the other side of the room, talking to some guy she had no business talking to."

Bobby grinned and chuckled. Garrett must have learned from Cowboy's move on Monika.

"She'd been checking me out as well," he said. "When I walked her way, she came right over, met me on the dance floor, and that was that. From that moment, we were two halves of one person."

Garrett talked about the good years. Her parents embraced him, although they knew only too well what Garrett and Kathy had in front of them.

Garrett told him he experienced some success repairing appliances, along with heating and air conditioning units. The two of them discussed moving somewhere new and him starting a business of his own. Kathy was born to be a schoolteacher.

"She finished at Maryland, got a master's in education at Pitt, and taught high school German in Harrisburg." He said the fact that she was Black but spoke German like a native only made her cooler.

They'd learned Kathy was pregnant the same day he was mugged, and she was gang raped and then beaten to death.

"I have to believe they thought they'd killed me that night in Harrisburg," Bensen said. "After I recovered, I mourned, hated, plotted. I went back to Minnesota.

"I took my own sweet time going back there, following them, getting to know their routines, learning who they were—stalking them, I guess." He took a drink from a cup of water. "The third one, DiStefano, was the first one who raped her. And then the other two raped her. And then Tisdale killed her—beat her to death."

Bobby told him he couldn't find any information about a rape.

"Not surprising," Prettyboy said. "The only honest man in that whole system was Rickoff, the medical examiner. I ambushed him after I was released from the hospital. I'd missed her funeral. He told me she'd been raped and that there were—How did he put it?—'multiple contributors.' *Contributors*. Interesting choice of words, right?"

Bobby approached his next line of questioning very carefully.

"Can I ask you some questions about the immediate aftermath of the original event?" he asked.

Prettyboy nodded and started in on his own.

"I was hurt worse than I'd originally thought," he said. "When I got out of the hospital, I called the Cobbs. They'd had to identify Kathy's body. The colonel told me the HPB had told them they didn't know where I was. They took her home to Pittsburgh before I'd been released. I had no chance to say goodbye."

"Wait," Bobby said. "They didn't know where you were? No one from the Harrisburg police ever interviewed you?"

Garrett shook his head. "Looking back, I thought it was strange. But when I was released from the hospital, I was a mess. It flew under my radar."

"Garrett," Bobby said, "I'm only an author, not a cop, but it seems you'd have been the first person they'd have wanted to talk to. When the wife gets murdered, the husband is the first suspect."

"I realized that later, Bobby," he said. "That's what helped me understand exactly who I was dealing with when I came back. First thing after the hospital, I went to HPB to see if I could get information about the investigation."

Bobby couldn't suppress the sad smile crossing his face. "Don't tell me," he said. "Someone told you the file was missing."

Garrett nodded. "Mmmm hmmm," he said, tight lipped. "Fucked up, right?"

They stared at one another for a moment. "Guess hindsight's always twenty-twenty, right?" Garrett asked. Bobby shook his head.

"I must ask, Garrett, Why didn't any of this come out at your trial? At the very least it would have reduced your sentence."

Prettyboy smiled, exhaled, and looked at his old friend.

"Once I finally confessed, the notion of a long life in prison never sounded all that great to me," he said. "But in here, I'm a big deal, a cop killer. The real bad guys on the row, they see me as some kind of hero. How fucked up is that?"

Garrett Bensen, hero cop killer, Bobby thought.

"I kept tabs on the cops, Tisdale and Sheffield. They'd meet up often with DiStefano. He was a snitch of theirs, another pair of hands when they needed it. They had some protection deal going on. DiStefano was pimping some girls. That's what I learned anyway. These were bad guys, except one had a badge and they all had guns." He took a deep breath and signaled for the guards to take him back to his cell. "I'm just so tired."

Bobby wasn't ready to go, but Prettyboy was clearly exhausted.

"I never realized Pennsylvania was so unenlightened about race," Bobby said.

Garrett laughed. "You'd think that stuff only happens in the South, but it can happen anywhere. And it does."

Bobby saw the energy empty out of his friend. *We haven't been at it that long*, he thought.

"There's a joke about Pennsylvania," Garrett said. "Philadelphia is in the east, Pittsburgh's in the west, and Alabama is in the middle," he said.

"I need to ask you about how you finally got caught, Garrett," Bobby asked. "You got away with this for several years."

"Next time, Cityboy," he said. "Maybe tomorrow, if you can stay one more day."

A guard unchained Garrett, and he walked him back to his cell on death row.

• • •

Bobby needed to get something to eat before shutting down for the night. The sky filled with menacing clouds. Warren waited outside the last door, caught Bobby on his way out.

"He won't tell you this, Bob, but he's sick," he said.

"Sick? What kind of sick?"

"He came in here, a young guy, with stage-two colon cancer. The commonwealth happily treated him, and the taxpayers happily paid for it, just so he could live long enough to be duly executed for his crimes," the warden said. "Here we are, twenty-some years later. I must tell you, Bob, sometimes the so-called justice system is completely incomprehensible."

He told Bobby that Garrett thought he'd be dead by now, but about a year and a half ago he learned the cancer was in remission. That was the good news. The bad news was the drug treatments left him with a serious liver infection—Hepatitis C.

"The cancer goes into remission, and he gets a life-threatening liver infection instead," Jim Warren said.

"And he can't really do anything about it," Bobby said, "because he's under a death sentence, and besides, the state can take credit for helping cure his cancer."

They looked at one another. Bobby wished there was something, anything, he could do or say.

"He gets worn out easily," Warren said. "Existing treatment of the infection hasn't had much effect. He figured he'd die naturally before having to take the needle. But our doc says it's different with the infection. There are some promising experimental treatments out there but, as a prisoner under a death sentence, he's not eligible. Fact is, though, as things stand right now, about two and a half months from today, Garrett Bensen will be dead."

"Did you know about his history?" Bobby asked.

The warden shook his head. "I hear so much bull-shit from these guys, it all becomes white noise in my head," he said. "I believe a lot of what Bensen says because, God help me, I think there's a good guy in there. It's easier to believe he did what he did because they did what they did to him and his wife. He might never have been caught if he'd just let things lie. Irony is a bitch."

Bobby stared at him for a moment, waiting for the punch line. "Meaning?" Bobby asked.

Jim Warren shook his head. "Sorry, Bob. He needs to tell you that part himself."

Chapter 11

Despite his previous experience, Bobby hit the Outback Steakhouse again. He sat at the bar and ordered wings, fries, and a blooming onion. Three bottles of Iron City washed down the fried food orgy. The beer helped everything he'd learned slosh around in his head like clothes in a washing machine. He needed to get home; he was eating terribly. If she knew, Lindy would be very upset.

The same guys who beat Garrett up twice in Germany clubbed him again in downtown Harrisburg and killed his wife. He never got to know his baby. He may have gotten his revenge—but at what cost? He was facing his own death, either from a rotten liver infection or lethal injection.

After he paid his bill and got behind the wheel of his rental car, Bobby resolved, if Garrett gave the word, he'd petition everyone who could possibly change the lethal injection outcome. That would at least let Garrett live or die on his own terms.

. . .

There were still pieces of the puzzle missing. Bobby needed to know how the killings of DiStefano, Sheffield, and Tisdale went down. Of course, he needed to understand why and how Garrett got caught. And he needed to learn more about the other alleged killings and, especially, more about Mr. Senator Ed Ianucci. Bobby couldn't shake the notion that Ianucci was a little too protective of this one case, as opposed to all the others he'd prosecuted.

He shook his head. *Something ain't right.*

Bobby returned to his room and spent the better part of the evening on the

phone with Bill Densmore.

"You told me you reached out to a friend in the Pennsylvania state legislature for a referral, right?"

"Right," Cowboy answered. "We went to law school together in Colorado before he moved east to work for his wife's family. He wasn't quite as influential then as he is today. At the time, I was only looking for someone to represent Prettyboy. Why?"

Bobby chose his words carefully, unsure how to broach something like this politically.

"I'm not able to reveal too much yet," he said. "I'm seeing Prettyboy again tomorrow. I need to clear with him what I can and can't talk about before he's executed. Speaking strictly hypothetically, does your old friend hold any sway in matters involving capital punishment?"

The line went silent. Cowboy started to chuckle, then laugh. Then, he started coughing.

"You okay?"

"I've been thinking about that guy since your visit," he said, after he stopped coughing. "He sits on the Pennsylvania Supreme Court, Bobby. That means he's got a hell of a lot of influence over matters like capital punishment. What, exactly, is on your twisted Brooklyn mind?"

The idea wasn't quite fully formed yet in Bobby's head. What he presented probably sounded disjointed to a linear thinker like Cowboy. Densmore offered a bunch of grunts, a few "uh huhs" and "hmmms," but he didn't play devil's advocate or anything like that. He mused about logistics, legal ethics, and interstate representation, but didn't touch any of the substance of Bobby's inquiry.

"See what you can find out when you visit with him tomorrow," Cowboy said. "Ask him if it's okay for you and me to start down this road. I don't want to reach out unless he's fully on board."

"I'll do it." Then Bobby asked, "Maybe when you do talk to your friend, you could take his temperature regarding Garrett's prosecutor—Ed Ianucci. He's now a state senator."

"A senator?"

"He parlayed his reputation as a badass prosecutor into a senate seat," he said. "And now he's running for governor as the tough-on-crime candidate. He and I are developing an . . . interesting kind of relationship."

They agreed to talk again after Bobby got additional information about the killings, Bensen's capture, and why no one on his legal team had sought a lighter sentence.

• • •

When Bobby walked out of his hotel the next morning, anticipating the short drive to SCI-Greene, he found all four tires of his rental car had been slashed. Two of the windows had been smashed, along with the windshield. A dead raccoon was laid out on the driver's seat. No one at the hotel had seen anything, but they helped him locate a replacement vehicle and put in a call to the state police.

Bobby moved under the porte cochere to make the call. He caught a glimpse of a black Honda SUV leaving the Hampton Inn lot. He felt like the driver was laughing. *Maybe I'm just paranoid.* He reminded himself: just because you're paranoid doesn't mean someone isn't out to get you.

He called to push back his appointment with Garrett. The warden was shaken by the turn of events.

"A dead raccoon?" Warren asked. "Seriously?"

"I guess they couldn't find a rat," Bobby said. "State cops are coming to collect evidence. Look for fingerprints."

"Or paw prints." Warren hesitated. "A dead raccoon."

Bobby had another contribution to an already bizarre conversation.

"I had a visitor the other evening."

"Do I really want to know about this?" Warren asked.

"Probably not," Bobby said. "Are you familiar with a weasel by the name of Tom Cavanaugh?"

There was silence on the other end of the line.

"You meet Tommy Cavanaugh and a couple of days later your car gets raccooned?" the warden asked. "Yes, I know who Tommy Cavanaugh is. He's Ed Ianucci's dirty hands."

Bobby nodded. "Got it," he said. "I'm going to be late today."

"I was about to call you off today anyway," Warren interrupted. "Garrett checked into the hospital unit late last night. Early indications are food poisoning, which makes zero sense. No one else had problems from last night's dinner."

Had they been in the same room at that moment; had they been able to see one another's faces, they probably would have stared at each other for as long as it took for the first one to call bullshit on these coincidental events.

"What kind of symptoms did he have?" Bobby asked.

"As far as I know, some bad stomach pains and a little blood in his vomit. What are you thinking?"

In one of Bobby's early short stories, poisoning food was part of the killer's MO, his method of operation.

He had done research on purposeful food poisoning. He wasn't an expert on the subject by any means, but it sounded like a low dose of arsenic.

"I wonder if someone's so bent out of shape by me being here that they'd try to kill Garrett."

"I don't know, Bob," Warden Warren said. "I can't see how this happens to one inmate, on the row, with my most trusted people involved," Warren said. "Feels like someone—you—may have kicked a hornet's nest. I'm sorry about today."

"I've got plenty to do, Jim," Bobby said. "Pencil me in for the same time tomorrow."

• • •

It rained all day. Bobby called Lindy, bounced a couple hundred things around with her, and spent the rest of the wet day waiting on state cops and rental car people while he banged the keys on his MacBook Pro.

• • •

When Bobby next saw Garrett, his color was a bit pale but mostly good. Bobby decided he wouldn't mention anything Warren had said about Garrett's health. Instead, he asked about the food poisoning.

"I don't know," Garrett said. "I had dinner like always. But later I got bad cramps and threw up blood, had the runs. They got me squared away in the hospital."

Bobby felt more certain about his arsenic theory. A larger dose could have been fatal.

"I read the newspaper article," Bobby started. "I've got additional questions about how you handled the crimes."

"TRIPLE HOMICIDE IN DOWNTOWN HARRISBURG"

By Micah Previn

In what HPB Chief Donald J. Porimski is calling the worst case of multiple homicides in Harrisburg history, police were directed to a back alley near the corner of Peffer Street and Fourth Street, where they found three bodies in the early hours of Wednesday morning.

"The three are HPB sergeant Cletus Tisdale, former HPB officer Arthur Sheffield, and Joseph DiStephano, a career criminal," HPB spokesperson Robert Bright said. "We're awaiting definitive word on the causes of death from the Dauphin County Medical Examiner." Bright told The Patriot-News there are currently no leads, and, as he put it, "There was almost no forensic evidence found at the scene.

Right now, we're not even sure if the crime occurred where the bodies were found."

DiStefano brought a long criminal history with him when he relocated from Brooklyn, New York, to Harrisburg in 1978. Since arriving in central Pennsylvania, he's faced charges of pandering, multiple counts of assault, breaking and entering, auto theft, and possession of a firearm. He spent almost two years of accumulated time in the Dauphin County Prison on Mall Road over his years in Harrisburg.

Arthur Sheffield joined the HPB in 1984 following eleven years as an Air Police officer with the United States Air Force. He was accused eight times of employing unnecessary force while making arrests before being terminated in 1986.

Cletus Tisdale had been a patrol sergeant since coming on board with HPB in 1985. Prior to joining the HPB he was an Air Police shift supervisor in Darmstadt,

West Germany. He grew up in Tennessee, and leaves behind a wife
and a daughter.

Police officials claim no knowledge regarding the nature of the
relationship, if any, between
DiStefano, the criminal, and Tisdale and Sheffield, current and
former police officers.

Bobby pushed the record button on his microcassette and leaned it against the Plexiglas room divider
under the screened opening. He nodded at Garrett.

"I stayed in Harrisburg about three months after
Kathy was murdered to see if they'd even make a show
of looking for the killer, or killers," Garrett started.
"Since all I had were suspicions, I mostly kept to myself."

Garrett told Bobby he returned to Minneapolis
after Kathy's parents told him to get on with his life
and not let himself become another victim.

"I hired on with a local HVAC service company as
a salesman, if you can believe it. Me, a salesman." He
laughed. "It left my nights and weekends free for the
completion of my . . . education."

Bobby waited for Garrett to keep talking, but Garrett wanted Bobby to lead him.

"In no conversation I've had with anyone close to
your case or in my review of the case file was there
mention of any murder weapon," Bobby said. He let

the statement hang in the musty air of the prison's interview room.

Garrett nodded and looked down at his manacled hands.

"I spent a lot of time learning how to handle and fire a gun," he said. "I joined a club in suburban Minneapolis and bought a couple handguns. I got pretty good at hitting the target. My anger got the best of me, and I decided that shooting those maggots would be letting them off easy." He paused.

"You're Jewish, Bobby. You ever hear of Krav Maga?"

Bobby nodded. He'd heard the words a long time ago, when he'd invested four years of his life in Tae Kwon Do training.

"It's an Israeli martial art," Garrett said. "I met a guy from Jerusalem at the gun club." He smiled at the memory. "His name was Ziv Modor. He'd relocated from Israel to New York and then Minneapolis after the war in '73. He went to college at Minnesota and became a pharmacist. We became friends. He became a mentor, so to speak. He was quite a bit older than me." Garrett sipped from a plastic cup of water.

"For the next year, Ziv taught me Krav Maga, which the Israeli Defense Force had incorporated into training for Mossad and Shin Bet's army," he said. "I was a motivated student. I attained a high level of proficiency. He told me I was equal to a fourth-degree black belt."

Prettyboy's hands had become lethal weapons. Unless there were guns involved, he could easily disable three or four untrained people, usually in under a minute. Bobby made a note to investigate Krav Maga and Shin Bet. He already knew Mossad was one of the most badass organizations in the world.

"So, you learned Krav Maga. Then?"

"Then I grew a beard, got a brush cut, and went back to Harrisburg."

Bobby took in a deep breath. He'd never heard anyone confess the details of a triple murder before.

"It was almost a year after everything had happened. I walked the streets around the neighborhood where we were attacked," he said. "I figured if they were there that night, maybe they hung out in that part of the riverfront."

"Not the most expeditious way to track down some douche bags you didn't even have a good description of," Bobby offered.

"What else could I do?" he asked. "A week into my hunt, I saw a familiar face in a small park on the riverfront. It was that medical examiner—Rickoff. It was about 9:30 at night. He sat in a folding chair with an easel, a canvas, and a bunch of tubes of paint. We struck up a conversation."

A medical examiner who paints, Bobby thought. *That guy will definitely show up in a Robert L. Kaminsky book.*

"I told him I wanted to find out who was responsible. He had told me Kathy was raped. No one else did. He also told me not to hold my breath waiting for anyone to solve Kathy's murder."

Bobby kept quiet. He thought, *It must have been hard being an ethical medical examiner inside an otherwise corrupt system.*

"I felt comfortable talking to him, so I just unloaded. I told him everything. I had nothing to lose," Garrett said. "Maybe I was stupid. I believed he would keep it to himself. At the time, I didn't think anything would come of it."

"What unlocked the door?"

"I told him what I heard just before the lights went out in Harrisburg, that it brought back memories of the beatings in Germany. 'Bubba.'

"Rickoff just shook his head and said, 'Tisdale. Cletus fucking Tisdale. Asshole calls everyone Bubba. He's just one of the worst of a whole bushel basket of rotten apples.' Then he told me about Sheffield, mentioned they ran with a creepy, little bottom-feeder named Joey DiStefano. Said they were responsible for all kinds of shit, but there was no one in the system who was clean enough or brave enough or high up enough to do anything about it. They were protected. That's the word he used: protected."

Protected? Bobby thought. *Maybe by a prosecutor, who later became a senator?*

• • •

Cletus Forrest Tisdale was born in Shelbyville, Tennessee, at a time when the town was known for two things: one, Tennessee Walking Horses; two, for being the birthplace of the founder of the Ku Klux Klan, Nathan Bedford Forrest.

Cletus's parents, J. D.—that would be Jefferson Davis—Tisdale, and his wife, Althea Stuart-Tisdale, brought their only child up to respect and observe the traditions of the Old South, including a love of sweet tea and a blind, deeply ingrained hatred for Black people who "infested" the Bedford County community.

As a child, Cletus demonstrated a social awkwardness, probably flowing from his helicopter mother, Althea. She was ever-present due to an irrational assuredness that, if she were to leave the boy alone for even a few minutes, he'd most certainly be attacked by persons of unknown race or origin simply because he was her perfect, pasty-White boy. He picked up on this maternal idiosyncrasy early on and absorbed it right into his DNA.

Cletus Tisdale discovered his future path and his own racist mindset at Shelby South High School. The biggest boy in ninth grade, Cletus accepted an invitation to join the Junior Knights of the KKK with the enthusiastic blessing of his parents.

As a member and eventually a leader of the JKs, Cletus participated in marches, ritual beatings of Black boys in the county, and the occasional cross burning. Not the brightest of lights, the crosses they burned sometimes mistakenly ended up in the front lawns of adult members of the Knights. Cletus took several beatings for these missteps, some of which came at the hands of his parents. Their boy needed to understand, to live their version of right from wrong.

As a high school senior, Cletus applied and was accepted into the Bedford County Sheriff's Explorers. There he got a taste of the power a uniform, badge, and handgun would afford him down the road. He'd already learned to handle and shoot a long gun from his father. Part of his Explorer training included achieving proficiency on a variety of handguns. Cletus liked handguns, and he grew very fond of the batons carried by Bedford County deputies.

After graduating in the lower half of his class, Cletus enlisted in the air force against the passionate wishes of his mother, who wanted her perfect boy to be a marine. The marine recruiter never made any promises to their recruits, but the air force staff sergeant told Cletus that he'd likely be eligible for Air Police training. That sealed the deal.

After basic training in San Antonio, then Air Police Academy training in the Florida panhandle, followed by service at two air force Reserve centers in Pittsburgh and Harrisburg, Pennsylvania, Cletus Tisdale arrived in Darmstadt attached to the 6910th Radio Group Mobile in late 1979, seven years after he enlisted.

Cletus spent six more years in the APs, attained the rank of E-6, technical sergeant, and returned to the USA with a German bride. His mother was thrilled that her son would be producing potentially perfect offspring—but it wouldn't be in Tennessee. Instead of coming home to Shelbyville, Cletus secured civilian employment with the Harrisburg Police Bureau.

• • •

Bobby was confused.

"You put all this together on the strength of being referred to as Bubba? Every redneck in America calls people Bubba."

"What can I tell you, Bobby? Stranger things." From then on, he told Cityboy, it was Garrett Bensen, patient predator, carefully closing in on his quarry.

"It actually took no time to track these assholes down," he said. "DiStefano was easy. He turned out to be the weakest link of the three. I watched him all day every day for over a week." He laughed. "The idiot scumbag was actually listed in the phone book."

Chapter 12

T*hank God for stupid criminals*, Bobby thought. *Even good cops had a tough time fighting and solving crime but for the fact that most criminals were just plain stupid.*

"I suspected sooner or later DiStefano would lead me to Sheffield and Tisdale, so I just watched and waited," Garrett said. "I learned patience from Ziv. In Krav Maga, even when you break it down into seconds, or fractions of seconds, waiting for the right moment is key."

Bobby thought back to something he'd read in Garrett's case file, and in some of the news accounts. All three bodies were found alongside a row of garbage cans in an alley near the intersection of North Third Street and Peffer in downtown Harrisburg. No weapon was recovered at the scene because none was necessary. There were three distinct causes of death. Tisdale was strangled. DiStefano's neck was broken. Sheffield died from a blow to the back of the head. There wasn't a drop of blood at the scene. Bobby looked at Garrett. Even with a confession, what could have possessed a jury to believe beyond a shadow of doubt he could take down three armed men with no weapon of his own? *Right*, Bobby thought. *A confession.*

"It had been a while, and they'd only seen me from behind. I'd changed my appearance enough from the night of the mugging. They never recognized me. Not until I reminded them who I was.

"I played drunk outside a German restaurant on Front Street. Kathy and I had eaten there a few times. I'd tracked them there earlier," he said. "My idea was to get them angry at me, then get them to follow me to a quiet place. Knowing Tisdale's tendencies, I took a gamble. If he had numbers, he'd try to teach me a lesson." He paused for a drink of water. Bobby had questions but didn't want to stanch Garrett's flow.

"When they came out of the restaurant, I acted drunk and stumbled into them. I rubbed dirty hands over their nice jackets. They cursed at me, but it was Sheffield who signaled the others to follow as I weaved up Front Street toward Peffer. I turned into an alley behind a pizza place near North Third Street. They followed along, just like sheep."

"Three against one," Bobby said. "And they were armed?"

Garrett smiled. "All carrying. But these sadistic bastards were more interested in pounding on some drunk loser than they were in killing anyone." He bit his lip. "Exception made for a young Black woman. I have to believe they had no idea she was pregnant. Not that it would have changed anything."

Bobby scribbled a few notations. If he was crystal clear on any of this, it was that anything about Kathy was still a fresh wound.

"Ziv's training was perfect. It took me no time to disable them," he said. No hubris, no attitude. He took another deep breath. He was getting tired again.

"Do you want to take a rest, Garrett?" Bobby asked. "I have more questions, but I don't want to . . ."

"I'm dealing with a little health thing," he said. "Give me a minute."

He raised his glass and looked at the camera. A guard came in with a pitcher of water and filled the plastic cup. He looked hard at Bobby before patting Bensen on the shoulder and leaving.

"I lifted DiStefano up and told him my name," Garrett said. "He didn't respond so I told him the date, the location, and the name of the woman he raped and killed. He was trying to comprehend what I was saying when Tisdale piped in. 'You remember, Joey. That hot little nigger gal we played with a few years back.'"

"He actually said that? out loud?" Bobby asked.

"Stupid criminals and stupid cops," Garrett said. "I kicked Tisdale in the ribs and returned my attention to DiStefano. He was scared. 'We didn't mean to kill her' he said. 'She was kicking and screaming and he— he pointed at Sheffield—he said we needed to shut her up.' I asked if he raped her. He didn't answer, but I knew. I'd heard enough, so I grabbed his hair and slammed the heel of my hand into the soft spot on the back of his neck. He was dead before he hit the ground."

Bobby looked away. *Assholes got what they deserved.* He wondered what the corrections officers listening in were thinking.

"Sheffield was Tisdale's lackey. He did what he was told and didn't have the brains to fight," Garrett said. "All he did was beg for mercy. I told him I was fresh out. I knew this move that separates the brain stem from the spine. He never knew what hit him."

Garrett Bensen, Bobby thought, *reporting the news.*

"I turned my attention to Tisdale," he said. "I shook and slapped him until he was awake. Told him my name was Garrett Bensen. That he'd jumped me and my girlfriend in Darmstadt. 'You remember that?' He looked at me. I pointed over at Sheffield. 'You and that dead piece of shit over there knocked me around again in Germany when I was walking back to my barracks with my girlfriend. You remember that? You remember her?' I asked. I started working on his organs, just like Ziv taught me. 'That girl you talked about a minute ago? She was my wife. She was pregnant.' He looked at me and said 'Pregnant, huh? Yeah, didn't know that at the time. I guess we got two for the price of one.' The asshole shit himself while I choked the life out of him. Didn't even put up a fight."

He took a drink.

"I watched him die." He paused. "I watched him die. It shames me now, but at the time, I found it a beautiful thing."

Garrett's narrative was matter of fact. So much so that Bobby forgot this middle-aged man was once a kid, once his roommate. He had once been Bobby's closest friend. He avenged the monumental injustice visited on him by three very bad people shielded by a corrupt system meant to protect people like him and Kathy.

Bobby tried to maintain eye contact but couldn't. He looked down, away. He put a tight smile on his face.

"That's why no weapon was found, no blood at the crime scene," Bobby said.

"I'm sure Rickoff figured out how they died. While it was all happening, I had a sense someone else might have been in that alley, but I never actually saw anyone. No witness ever came forward. The trial got a lot of publicity. But in the end, they didn't need any of it."

Bobby leaned back, looked at his old friend.

"You believe Rickoff knew?"

Garrett smiled. "Of course he knew. I also believe he slept just fine after he sliced up those three assholes." He paused. "I stayed for a few weeks after, waiting to see how they'd go after the cop killer."

"Are you going to make me ask?"

"It was big news for a couple of days, then nothing. Absolutely nothing."

He guzzled down his water, exhaled slowly.

"That's the first time I ever told that story to anyone."

"Garrett," Bobby began. "I need to know how and why you finally got caught. You'd planned everything. You were a free man for three years. What happened?"

Garrett diverted his eyes. Bobby waited for him to tell it his way.

"I thought about what I'd done for a long time. Every day." He fiddled nervously with his thumbs. "I worked, I went to school, I even tried dating. But what did I have to offer someone else? My head was a mess, and I . . . I guess I felt guilty about killing those pieces of garbage."

None of that surprised Bobby. The Garrett Bensen he remembered was not a cold-blooded killing machine. It wasn't how he was wired.

"I got diagnosed with colon cancer after I came back home to Minneapolis," Garrett said. "Early '93."

Bobby hung his head.

"I was at rock bottom in every possible way," Garrett said. "I had to get right with myself, had to get right with God. I figured I could at least own the shit I'd done, let things play out in prison. I learned how things worked. If I got caught, I'd plead guilty, go to prison, and live until I died."

"Let me get this straight," Bobby said. "You gave yourself up?"

"I guess so." Garrett tore the corner off his small napkin, balled it up, fiddled with it some more. "I cut myself off from my sister. I didn't want her to deal with any fallout from this. I stopped calling, stopped returning her calls, got mad at her when she showed up at my door one weekend. That was hard. She was all I had left in the world. She is a very good person. She didn't need to own any of my bad shit."

Bobby tried to comprehend Prettyboy's state of mind.

"You had effectively gotten away with this," Bobby said. "How long after you came home to Minnesota did you hatch this scheme?"

"I know you can't understand," Garrett said. "I was plenty messed up; I had nothing to live for. I thought about ending it myself, but I didn't have the nerve."

That's fucked up, Bobby thought.

Garrett smiled, laughed. "I was a few years into my sentence when I realized it wasn't going to happen any time fast. I started wondering why I didn't just head for the hills."

"I'm not here to judge you, brother," Bobby said. "I wasn't in your skin and didn't lose what you'd lost. Go ahead. Tell me how it went down."

Garrett shrugged. "It wasn't any kind of grand plan. I phoned the Harrisburg Police Bureau with an anonymous tip. Less than two hours later, I was in custody in Minneapolis. Next day, they shipped me back to Harrisburg. The rest you know."

"How bad is the cancer now?"

Garrett shook his head and smiled.

"God works in mysterious ways, Bobby," he said. "When I gave myself up, I thought I'd be long gone by now, but then the cancer went into remission. Now it's some liver infection. It probably won't kill me before the state does, but I'm told there's no treatment for it. Not in here anyway."

Bobby paced around the small interview room. Garrett sat, drank water, waited.

Bobby had ceased taking meaningful notes. He needed to get to a place where he could transcribe all of this.

"You have to understand," Garrett said. "I made it impossible for them to do anything other than what they did. I copped to Tisdale, Sheffield, and DiStefano. I couldn't even fake remorse. The lawyers didn't have much to work with. That they tried to hang those other murders on me told me the system, especially the DA's office, was still a cesspool. In terms of the three I did commit; I got a fair trial and the right sentence." He licked his lips and emptied his water cup. "Figured I'd be gone by now. Turns out prison health care isn't as bad as prison food."

"Prettyboy . . . I'm really sorry about the infection," Bobby said. It was time for a Filthy Five Hail Mary.

"Densmore thinks there's a chance for you to get clemency. Not a reversal or a pardon, but a bump down to life. You could at least live until the infection kills you."

Garrett smiled. Bobby's heart ached. He still loved that smile.

"I love you guys for wanting to do something," Garrett said. "But why would I want to live like this? Kathy is dead. The baby is dead. I killed three people. I have an infection that's going to kill me some day. Nothing changes any of it. Let it play out. Just write the book, tell the story, let people know that Kathy Bensen was a terrific woman, a terrific teacher, would have been a terrific mother. Let them know who I used to be. Maybe it'll set things right with my sister." His eyes filled with tears.

This time it was Bobby who signaled for the guard.

• • •

In Harrisburg, a phone rang.

"Ianucci," he answered.

A voice on the other end spoke long and without a break, other than for Ianucci's "uh huh, uh huh, uh huh" responses.

When the call ended, Ianucci summoned Tommy Cavanaugh.

"We need to get this asshole Kaminski out of the picture. You've been keeping eyes on him?"

"Yes," Kavanaugh answered.

"Good," Ianucci said. "Here's what I want you to do."

Chapter 13

Bobby's next stop was home. He packed and checked out of the Hampton Inn. He left the prison and headed straight up I-79 toward Pittsburgh International Airport.

While making notes into his voice recorder, he noticed a vehicle coming up behind him way too fast for the right lane. Bobby hit the gas, but the vehicle, a black SUV, cut to the left lane and rode for a few seconds in his blind spot. Bobby tapped his brakes and considered gifting the driver with the international "fuck you" sign when the SUV sped up alongside the car. Bobby heard two shots. He jammed on his brakes, but the damage was done. He lost control of the car.

Bobby turned the wheel hard to the right and flipped the Kia off the road. The car came to rest on the driver's side, just like that roll decades earlier in Darmstadt. This time, instead of landing on the steps of a police station in Germany, he landed in a shallow, grassy ditch. He was wearing a seatbelt and was able to open the passenger door. He felt dizzy, nauseous. He touched his forehead and found a nasty gash, along with a sharp pain in his right arm. The airbag had deployed.

He tumbled out to his knees and looked for the SUV, but it was long gone. A red F-150 stopped to make sure Bobby was okay. The driver called for assistance. Bobby wanted to let it go and hitch a ride to the airport. But he would miss his flight; it would be hours until the next one. His arm stung with pain; he had been hit just under his left shoulder. He made a half-true report to the troopers who came to investigate. With the car resting on the driver's side window, the troopers figured it was a one-car accident.

He knew how the story would sound if he started blaming a random Pennsylvania senator. He decided against naming names of people who were upset with him for sticking his nose in an old capital murder case. He didn't want to get carted off to some state mental institution. He claimed to be visiting a friend in Waynesburg and was heading to the airport. He had no idea who did this. Maybe it was some random road rage thing.

"They were in a black SUV," he said. "I didn't know I'd been shot until it was over."

Paramedics took him to Washington Hospital to be treated. The ER doctor talked him into a scan to make sure his head was okay. It was another day and a half before he could get to PIT and catch a flight to Tampa.

• • •

Lindy met him at TSP and gave him a love-fueled ration of indignation for everything that had happened to him thus far on this road trip of his.

"I love you Bobby K., but this is not how a middle-aged man researches a damn book," she said. "These assholes shot you!"

"It's just getting interesting, Lin," he said. "And very personal. And it's starting to really piss me off."

Lindy knew who he was and what he needed to do. Bobby walked her through everything since the last time they'd talked. After he'd gotten it all out, he chalked this latest episode up as just another dead raccoon, compliments of Ed Ianucci and his gang of crooked assholes.

• • •

August 2016

Bobby spent his time at home recuperating. He worked up a comprehensive outline for his first creative non-fiction book; his working title: *The Filthy Five: A Tale of Friendship, Murder, and Redemption.* He hoped he could make the redemption part happen. He stayed in touch with Farmboy, Cowboy, and Fatboy regularly.

They were in a holding pattern—then Jim Warren called.

"Bad news, my friend. Barring any miracles," he said. "Garrett Bensen will be executed by lethal injection one week from Friday. I'm assuming you will be in attendance?"

Bobby collapsed into his living room recliner. He studied the shining waters of the Gulf from the eleventh floor of their beachfront condo.

"I thought we had until September."

"We did, but not anymore," Warren said. "Ianucci held a presser late last night. He convinced a state superior court judge that Bensen needed to die sooner rather than later."

"He can do that?"

"He can, and he did," he said. "Bensen's been on the row for over twenty-three years. This will be Pennsylvania's first execution in a very long time so there's a lot of media interest. Will you be there?"

Not a lot of people line up to watch someone die, but Bobby would be there. And so would Bill Densmore, C. W. Allebaugh, and Johnny Lee—unless Warden Warren objected. Bobby popped the question.

"In any other instance," Warren said. "I'd stand firm on who could or could not witness an execution at my facility. But there aren't many names on Garrett's list. If your friends want to be there, I won't object." He hesitated. "Can't know what Ianucci might do."

"Please pardon my language, but fuck Ed Ianucci," Bobby said.

Bobby told the warden about his trip from Waynesburg to Pittsburgh.

"I know you're not making this stuff up," Warren said. "Maybe you should take a step back before something really bad happens."

Warren had no way of knowing that Bobby Kaminsky had never been very good at taking steps backward.

"I grew up a lower-middle-class kid in Brooklyn," Bobby said. "I'm not a tough guy, but this bullshit pisses me off. It makes me believe that someone—Senator Ianucci, for example—is scared shitless of what might come out. Sorry, Jim, but it's against my nature to step back."

"Just take care of yourself, Bob," Warren said. "I don't want to have to go to your funeral, okay?"

Bobby thanked him and pressed his luck. The Filthy Five had a plan for Garrett's going away party. Warren laughed out loud.

"Permission granted.," he said. "I just hope no TV stations pick that up and run with it."

Bobby called Allebaugh, who was ecstatic. Bobby hoped Bensen would be okay with it. It was now eleven days until Prettyboy's date with the needle.

• • •

Bobby called *The Harrisburg Patriot-News* to see if he could connect with Micah Previn, the reporter who covered Garrett's case. Good reporters never forget a story of consequence. They often have interesting observations that don't make it into print or police files. Bobby liked to talk to reporters because they were often as close to objective as humans get. Micah Previn still lived in the Harrisburg area and still reported for *The Patriot-News.*

"Garrett Bensen," Previn said. "I heard he's going to die soon. Guy should get a medal, not the needle."

Bobby asked if there was anything Micah could add to Benson's story.

"A couple of things. I always found it interesting that no one from Tisdale's family attended a minute of Bensen's trial. He was married and had a daughter, but neither the wife nor the daughter was at the trial. They wouldn't talk to me or to any other reporters, even after Bensen was sentenced."

"Did the others have family at the trial?" Bobby asked.

"Sheffield was divorced with no kids. His ex-wife was in Maryland. She had no interest in 'Artie the asshole,' as she called him. DiStefano's mother was in a memory care facility in Brooklyn. She's probably long gone by now."

Micah paused, remembering something.

"I can't be a hundred percent sure," he said. "I think Tisdale's widow may still be alive. A German gal if I remember correctly. Not sure where she is. I can try to run her down."

Bobby said he'd try himself first. If he needed help, he'd reach out.

"Do you know the widow's name?" Bobby asked.

Previn rustled through some notes.

"Got it! Yeah," he said. "Her name is Charlotte," he said, turning a page on an old notepad.

Bobby smiled. Tisdale had brought himself back the busty German *gasthaus* waitress.

"You going to the execution?" Previn asked.

"Absolutely," Bobby said. "You?"

"Nope," he said. "He eliminated three pieces of crap no one misses. My whole career here has been focused on crime, cops, and courts. I can tell you with absolute certainty; Harrisburg is way better off today for being rid of those assholes. What Garrett Bensen did, is he lit the fuse on a purge of the entire department. If you ask me, they should build a statue of him." Micah hesitated for a moment. "You know . . ." he said, and then paused again.

"Right, you said a couple of things bothered you." Bobby said.

"I'm not sure they ever cleared that girl's homicide," he said. "Bensen's wife."

"Double homicide," Bobby said. "She was pregnant." Bobby wasn't ready to tell Micah Previn that she was raped.

"That's right. I need to take a fresh look at those three cases Ianucci tried to bundle in with Bensen's."

"What are you thinking?" Bobby asked. He heard Micah breathe on the other end of the line.

"My guess—I'd have to look it up—at the time there were maybe thirty unsolved homicides in HPB's cold case file."

"So, why those particular three?"

"Exactly."

They agreed to talk again.

Bobby flipped open his laptop and searched for Charlotte Tisdale.

• • •

Bobby's memory landed on the notion that whether he'd ever admit it, or even remember it, Bill Densmore would always be indebted to Charlotte Tisdale. When she wasn't bringing GIs beer at Der Grosse Hund, she was matchmaking local girls with soldiers or airmen she thought might make decent husbands. No one had a remote shot at getting to Charlotte; she was spoken for. They didn't know that the American who would bring her home would be Air Police Staff Sergeant Cletus Tisdale.

Charlotte was short, busty, with jet-black hair, and a Marilyn Monroe birthmark on the left side of her nose. She always smelled like honey. She smiled at everyone but kept the GIs at arm's length. The barkeep, Gustav, was taciturn, generally unfriendly, efficient, and not too thrilled about serving obnoxious American troops. He was protective of Charlotte and Gisele, his other waitress. They flirted mercilessly with everyone, but at closing time, they always stayed behind.

...

Bobby would always be indebted to a fellow would-be author who gave him a valuable piece of advice when the two happened to be in a seminar focusing on writing crime fiction.

"You have to get the small details right so the reader will believe the big lie," he said. "Don't ever think of research as some minor thing. Even the smallest details matter." This nugget had served Bobby well in his writing career. He actually came to enjoy searching out what others might view as arcane minutiae.

With help from the internet, Bobby managed to locate Charlotte Tisdale in Sarasota. She was living with her daughter, her daughter's husband, and a couple of grandchildren. She'd be sixty-four years old on her next birthday. Bobby drove up from Naples. They lived in a small, tastefully landscaped Florida home half a block off Bahia Vista Road near Sarasota's Amish enclave.

Charlotte was nothing like he remembered. But who is after thirty years? She was welcoming and interested when he told her he wanted to talk about some guys who used to be in love with her.

"I'm sorry, Mr. Kaminsky," she said. She poured two glasses of Mosel wine, even though it was still a bit before noon. "I remember the Dog, of course, but I can't place you. When were you in Darmstadt?"

Bobby decided to see right off the bat if there was any water in this well.

"It was the early '80s," he said. "I didn't know your husband." Her face went to stone.

"I'm sorry that I did. Except for my daughter, that bastard gave me nothing but pain and misery. He's been dead a long time. He is of no importance to me. I have Christa, and I have my grandchildren. I'm in America, and we're all citizens. As far as Cletus is concerned, he is nothing but shit on the bottom of my shoe." She took a sip of her wine. "I'm sorry. I don't usually talk like this. That's an expression Cletus used often when talking about Black people."

Bobby took in a deep breath. "Please forgive me; I'm here to ask you some painful questions. An old friend is scheduled to die soon for the murder of your husband and two others in Harrisburg."

Her eyes widened. "Garrett Bensen? He's alive?"

"He is," Bobby said. "But only for nine more days."

"Well, just so you know," she said, "Garrett Bensen did me, Christa, and the world a big favor. I wish they wouldn't . . ." She poured more wine and sat up straight. "Why exactly are you here, Mr. Kaminsky? What do you want from me?"

"First, please call me Bobby, or Bob, Charlotte, and I need to explain some things."

"I know exactly what my late husband and those pigs did to that boy and his wife," she said. "Those three deserved what they got."

Bobby sat up straighter. "You do," he said. Not a question.

"Yes, I do." she said. "The three of them came back to our house that night, drunk, of course, like always, bragging about how they'd 'taken care of' a young White man and a Black woman who was with him. 'Not in our town,' they'd said. They probably thought I was asleep. Mean, nasty. Artie Sheffield was Cletus's partner until he left the Bureau. Said she was 'tasty.' DiStefano, that criminal, said they should do that every week. Made me sick. I don't know how they got away with that."

"How did you know who they were talking about?" Bobby asked.

"I'm not the smartest person in the world, but I'm not stupid either," she said. "It was in the paper and on TV the next morning. Harrisburg is a small town. Mr. Kaminsky, I'm sorry. Bob. These men were awful."

Bobby excused himself and asked to use the bathroom. He needed to catch his breath. It was hearsay, but she could still be a credible witness. A source, at least. He returned. She picked right up.

"I left Harrisburg soon after Cletus was killed. I put him in the ground, signed papers for his pension, and I left. He had been an abusive drunk since Germany. I don't know why I ever married him."

"You got here, and you have the rest of your family."

She walked to a window that overlooked a swimming pool.

"I had been here a few years when a friend from Harrisburg called to tell me they'd arrested someone named Garrett Bensen," she said. "I didn't make any connection of Cletus's killer to what they all talked about that night."

Bobby started to ask another question, but she wasn't finished.

"I didn't remember Garrett Bensen from Darmstadt. I don't remember most of the GIs from back then. I followed the trial in the papers. I didn't say anything to the media. They called all the time. Vultures—except that one reporter from the newspaper. What was his name?"

"Previn," Bobby said. "Micah."

"Micah," she repeated. "He was nice, considerate. But still, I had nothing to say to any of them. Most are vultures."

"I hope this doesn't offend you," Bobby said. "Why didn't you say something?"

She put up her hand. Her eyes filled with tears.

"Cletus was dirty," she said. "He was a bad policeman in a bad department. He had a lot of enemies. When they told me he and the others had been killed I had no idea who might have done it. It could have been anyone. He had hurt so many people." She swallowed back the painful memories. "I don't care who killed him. Christa and I, we couldn't get out of that awful place fast enough."

Bobby pondered whether anyone outside of Ianucci and the Harrisburg criminal justice system would make noise if Garrett's sentence got commuted.

Charlotte was finished. She was exhausted. He'd dug up some unpleasant memories in this woman's past. He felt badly, but not too badly. Bobby asked if he could keep in touch. She said that would be fine. As he left, she put a hand on his arm.

"That girl, she was pregnant?"

He nodded. "They'd just found out that day."

She sighed. "What awful men," she said. "I didn't do anything then. Is there anything I can do now?"

Bobby smiled. She had no idea how much she'd already done.

"I suppose you could send the governor of Pennsylvania a letter and tell him what you told me," Bobby said. He put his hands on her shoulders. "You know, we were all in love with you back then."

She smiled, shook her head. "No, you weren't. You were just boys. You were in love with these," she said, lifting her bosom.

He leaned down, gave her a hug, and kissed her on the cheek. They said their goodbyes. After all those years, she still had her German accent. And, to Bobby's delight, she still smelled like honey.

Chapter 14

Two days later, Bobby flew to New York to formally pitch *The Filthy Five* to the editorial team. They loved his outline and were all in. His pitch was interrupted by a call from Jim Warren.

"This morning," he said. "I get a call from someone who works for an associate justice on the state supreme court. He faxed me a notice, staying Bensen's execution for fourteen days. The PDLE, that's the Pennsylvania Department of Law Enforcement, is investigating some new information, stuff that never made it into the trial or into any of the state-mandated appeals. I can't help but wonder how a certain senator is responding to this little nugget of news."

"Probably banging around like a drunk squirrel," Bobby offered.

Charlotte had taken Bobby's offhand suggestion seriously. She'd written a detailed email to the governor's office regarding the night of Kathy Bensen's murder and Garrett's beating.

"You know," he said, "if I've learned anything in over twenty-eight years in this job, if something is going to happen, it's always going to happen days before the scheduled execution. A witness materializes out of nowhere, new evidence surfaces. Testimony gets recanted. When someone's life is on the line, even someone who's confessed to killing a cop, people want to do something."

Bobby played skeptic. "Everyone directly involved in this case is either Ianucci, Bensen, or dead. What changed?"

"According to McCarthy, Tisdale's wife was interviewed by police exactly once, for only four minutes, after her husband and cronies turned up dead," he said. "She left the state weeks after her husband was killed and didn't attend a single minute of the trial."

Bobby reported his visit with Charlotte Tisdale to Warden Warren.

"You convinced her to get involved?" he asked.

"Far from it," Bobby said. "She asked what she could do. I told her to write the governor. I never thought she would actually do it—or that it might really matter."

"You visited with Micah Previn, right?" he asked.

"Phone call, no visit," Bobby corrected.

"Tomato, tomahto," he said. "Previn reviewed his notes and contacted the detectives who investigated the murders. There were two separate notations about someone who may have been in the vicinity of where the murders took place."

"A witness?" Bobby asked. "After all this time, a fucking witness?"

"I said *may* have been in the vicinity. There's only a witness if the witness is identified, found, and has anything to add," he said. "But yes, there *may* be a fucking witness."

Cityboy reminded himself that Garrett did say he thought someone else might have been in the alley that night.

"I'm coming up in a couple days," Bobby said. "I need to talk to McCarthy. Maybe Previn again." Mostly, he needed to talk to Garrett about what this flurry of information might mean for his future.

"Would it be possible for me to talk with Garrett's doctor?"

"Doc Gable," Warren said. "He's a good guy, but technically, at least, that would be up to him, and Garrett, actually."

"Wednesday then," Bobby said, ignoring the warden's caveats and noting the meeting in his calendar.

• • •

Garrett's skin color had yellowed since the last time Bobby saw him. He slept a lot, even through some meals. Jim Warren had told Bobby to speed up his trip.

"He might be in sepsis," Warren said.

Bobby snatched a seat on a United Airlines flight out of Tampa that Monday. It arrived in Pittsburgh mid-afternoon. He picked up a rental and drove right to Waynesburg, bypassing Al McCarthy for the moment.

• • •

Nicholas Gable, MD, was overseer of Waynesburg's healthcare operation. It included six beds, a full-time lab, a morgue, a pharmacy, two offices, two nurses, two technicians, and a small but well-equipped surgery.

Specialists passed through whenever they were needed. On this day, Bobby met Alan Webb, MD, Garrett's infectious diseases guy. Webb was affiliated with Allegheny General Hospital in Pittsburgh. Jim Warren had ensured that Garrett had signed the necessary HIPAA releases, allowing the doctors to share his information with Bobby. Bobby's first question for the doctors was about Garrett's colon cancer.

"All the initial scans and biopsies indicated a growth in the colon," Dr. Gable said. "Despite his best efforts not to be treated, he received excellent care here. It's why he went into remission."

Bobby offered Gable a side-glance. "What does that mean, 'despite his best efforts not to'"?

The doctors shared a look. "No harm," Webb said. "It's been years."

"When Garrett Bensen arrived here, which was actually before my time, he knew he had colon cancer, but he didn't want the physician to treat it," he said.

"It was treated anyway, right?" Bobby asked.

Gable nodded. "According to the file," he said. "Not

only did he receive treatment, but the prosecutor demanded the medical team do everything possible to keep him alive so he could . . . receive the full extent of the verdict provided by the jury and the punishment handed down by the judge."

Bobby sat down. He was silent. The physicians shared occasional glances with one another.

"Mr. Kaminsky," Doc Gable began, but Bobby waved him off.

"I just need to understand this," he said. "Ianucci demanded Garrett be treated so he could be executed. We're going back decades here."

"A few things, sir. Just so you know, we don't consider a patient's record when providing care," said Dr. Gable. He was an internal medicine specialist by trade but a primary care physician in his current role. "That said, Garrett Bensen presented as a decent guy and, considering his condition, a mostly model patient. Can't say that about all the life forms we see over here."

"Mostly?" Bobby asked. "Is he difficult in any particular manner?"

Webb took this one.

"It's entirely possible he contracted Hepatitis C here, in the prison health facility. With this kind of infection, we can't always identify actual causation. Could be from a transfusion, from unsanitary tattoo tools, even sharing a razor with someone carrying the virus but showing no symptoms."

"Perhaps in different circumstances there's more

that could be done for him," Gable said. "There are trials on some promising treatments, but as a capital prisoner, a confessed and convicted cop killer, no less, it's out of the question."

Bobby nodded. "He told me he expected to be dead by now," he said. "Some things are happening with his case that could push his execution out or might even lead to a commutation."

The doctors looked at each other.

"I guess I shouldn't have said anything," Bobby began, "but Jim Warren told me the governor is—"

Gable stopped him.

"The warden's job is of little consequence with regard to the medical services here," he said. "Our . . . charter, if you will, under existing law, is to provide all necessary care so inmates can fulfill their debt to the state. Senator Ianucci wasted no time once he got elected, adding language to existing statutes governing healthcare in prisons. Current law essentially mandates staff healthcare providers do everything necessary and possible to keep prisoners alive so they can serve their full sentences. In the case of capital prisoners, like Garrett Bensen, short of killing someone to meet that mandate, that's what we do. We bring in specialists all the time. The costs are astronomical. But we're sworn—"

"Hang on a second, Nick," Dr. Webb interrupted. "What exactly are you looking for from us, Mr. Kaminsky?"

"I want to know find out, in the unlikely event Garrett Bensen is released, or if his sentence is commuted for whatever reason, whether he'd have a chance at any sort of decent life, based on his condition," Bobby said.

"The infection is very serious," said Dr. Webb.

"You need to understand something," said Dr. Gable. "This case is complicated. The state of Pennsylvania, in some manner of thinking, might have contributed to Garrett Bensen's Hepatitis C. He had colon cancer when he arrived. There are some dark side effects to treating that."

Bobby smiled and shook his head. "Let me see if I get this." He paced a tight circle in the prison dispensary office. "Care he received in prison managed to put his cancer into remission, but part of that outcome is that he may die from a side effect of the treatment? All due respect, gentlemen, that's nuts!"

Dr. Webb appeared to be uncomfortable. "I don't want to contradict my colleague," he said. "Neither of us can really say with certainty whether the treatment contributed to the infection. Unfortunately, he's not eligible for any of the new protocols being tested around the nation. Unless . . ."

"Unless he somehow manages to get out of prison before either the state or the infection kills him?" Bobby finished for him. "No offense, docs, and I know you guys have no role in prison public policy matters, but that's fucking ridiculous."

The two doctors said nothing.

Bobby shook hands with Webb and Gable. He thanked them for their time and candor. They'd given him more information than was permissible under HIPAA protocols.

Cityboy Bobby Kaminsky decided then and there he would do everything he could to change the current trajectory of Prettyboy's life.

• • •

Detective Ernest Cleaveland wore a grim expression. He strode purposefully down a corridor in the Pennsylvania statehouse in Harrisburg. Tall, fit, and well dressed, Cleaveland had been anticipating this for years—decades, in fact. He was ready. He'd already briefed his CO, the Chief of Detectives, and the Chief of the Harrisburg Police Bureau. He didn't mind telling the whole story again. After all, this was criminal justice.

The governor's chief of staff sat behind a cluttered desk in a small, unmarked statehouse office Governor Tom Hill maintained for quiet meetings with legislators, lobbyists, and media. Weldon Pepper didn't want to attract any attention, especially from the media, unless and until there was something of what he viewed as affirmative substance on a sensitive matter. The scheduled execution of a death-row inmate who may not deserve to die is one such example of a very sensitive matter.

"Thanks for meeting me here, Mr. Cleaveland," Pepper said.

"Detective Cleaveland," he said. "And thank *you* for meeting with me."

"This case has grown new wrinkles," Pepper said. "First, we received an interesting communication from the widow of one of Benson's victims. Then, a respected journalist hints at a possible witness to a decades-old crime. How old were you—a teenager?"

"I was fifteen when Garrett Bensen was jumped by three men in that alley," Detective Cleaveland said. "I spoke to my captain and my chiefs yesterday. As you know, Harrisburg is a much different city today and the HPB is a model police department compared with what it was. What happened back then wouldn't happen today. It couldn't. No rogue cops. We're not perfect, but stuff like that just doesn't happen anymore."

"Frankly, none of that matters. The big question," Pepper said. "Hell, the only question is why didn't you come forward at the time of the crime or later, after Bensen was captured, or even when he went on trial?"

"That's simple," Cleaveland said. "I wasn't here before, during, or right after either his capture or Bensen's trial. Three years after I witnessed the crime, I graduated from high school and got a football scholarship to West Virginia University. I'd pushed the events of that night far back in my mind. Until I read a news story this week about the search for a possible witness to a triple homicide that took place twenty-seven years ago, I'd all but forgotten the whole thing."

Pepper placed a copy of the piece Micah Previn had pushed into *The Patriot-News* onto the desk. The headline was posed as a question:

"A WITNESS TO 1989 MURDERS?"

Confessed murderer Garrett Bensen is scheduled to die by lethal injection at the Pennsylvania State Penitentiary in Waynesburg at one minute past midnight on Friday, August 23.

Bensen confessed to the murders of former police officer Arthur Sheffield, police sergeant Cletus Tisdale, and Joseph DiStefano, a career criminal with a long record of both felony and misdemeanor offenses.

The murders took place in 1989 in an alley behind a row of retail stores and restaurants near the corner of Peffer and North Third Streets.

Bensen has been on death row since his conviction in 1994.

A review of case files from the three murders indicated the

```
possible existence of a witness
to the crimes for which Bensen was
later convicted.
    The witness, possibly a child at
the time, was never interviewed and
has never been identified. Anyone
with knowledge of this witness is
asked to contact the Harrisburg PB
as soon as possible.
```

The article carried additional background, including references to Garrett's mugging and Kathy's murder. Accompanying the story were pictures of Garrett, Kathy, Ed Ianucci, Tisdale, Sheffield, and DiStefano. Several calls came into the hotline, but none panned out. As fate would have it, the actual witness was employed in the HPB's major crimes unit.

"I was just a kid. Scared out of my head. Not because of what I'd seen but because I was out roaming the waterfront when I should have been home in bed," Cleaveland said. "The truth is, Mr. Pepper, I was way more afraid of my grandmother than the HPB."

Weldon Pepper smiled. The detective wasn't finished.

"I didn't read newspapers or watch news when I was a kid," he said. "But I still knew what I was told clearly and often while I was growing up: the HPB was not . . . let's just call it especially racially sensitive at that time. As a Black boy, I was taught to avoid all unnecessary interaction with the police."

"I understand," the chief of staff said.

Detective Cleaveland shifted uncomfortably in the slat-backed chair.

"It was several years before Bensen stood trial and got sentenced. I played football in high school. Good enough to get a scholarship to Morgantown. I played football while I obtained a degree in criminal justice. The trial happened during that time. None of that was on my radar until I read this." He pointed at the article.

"You remember what you saw that night," Pepper said.

"After I read this article, it all came flooding back, like the Susquehanna after a heavy rain. Mr. Pepper. I will never forget that night. I was twelve to fifteen yards from where it happened. I was right there."

For the third time in two days, the detective recounted the story.

"Bensen stumbled into the alley. Looked to me like he was drunk, or maybe on drugs. Let's just say he appeared incapacitated. The three of them followed. One of them took out a gun. The big one, Tisdale I think, told him to put it away." He paused. "That was a mistake."

"How's that?" asked Pepper.

"One of the others put his hands on Bensen and in less than a minute, all of them were down. This guy took all three down so fast. You talk about being in the wrong place at the wrong time—I was frozen. I wanted to go home to my grandmother, but I couldn't leave.

"I couldn't tell anything about their injuries. I watched Bensen talk to each of them, close, one on one. When he was finished . . ." the detective swallowed. "He killed each one with his bare hands." He looked deeply into Pepper's eyes. "They made a mistake when they picked on him. They made a bigger mistake when they didn't shoot him. This guy? He was one badass dude."

"Do you remember anything they said?" Pepper asked.

"One of them dropped an n-bomb. DiStefano, a real piece of garbage, said something about 'not meaning to kill the girl.' I assume now he was referring to Bensen's wife. Dude was married to a Black girl when that was definitely not cool in Harrisburg."

"I'll probably need to talk to you again, Detective," Pepper said, standing up. "Right now, I need to get to Waynesburg and visit Mr. Bensen. He's not doing very well, health-wise."

Detective Cleaveland shook hands again with Weldon Pepper. "Bensen still confessed to killing three people. For better or worse, one of them was a cop."

"Yes," said Pepper. "But your story could mean what he did that night in that alley might constitute manslaughter, maybe even self-defense. None of this came out at trial or in any of his appeals. As far as the politics go, which is where my interests are, the governor needs to be on the right side of this, no matter what that side turns out to be."

Detective Cleaveland turned to leave.

"One thing, Detective," Pepper said, "I don't know yet how this is going to play out. I assume at some point you'll either be asked to report what you know or will, as a matter of conscience, desire to make what you saw public. I would ask, if possible, you hold onto this information, at least for a few days."

Cleaveland nodded. "I'll do what I can."

Chapter 15

In his office next door to Senator Ianucci's, an angry Tom Cavanaugh ripped a burner phone from a drawer and punched in a number.

"Fouser."

"You know who this is?"

"Yep."

"Listen closely," Cavanaugh said. "You're being paid good money—cash money—to control the situation down there. You like money, right?"

"The money is fine, it helps with my daughter's medical bills, but I don't know what more you or your boss want me to do," he said. "I keep you informed about their conversations. That is exactly what you asked me to do."

"Yeah, well, you need to do more," Cavanaugh said.

"I already did more," Fouser said. "I helped your people run Kaminsky off the road between here and Pittsburgh. I may have only driven but they shot him, and they put him in the hospital. It's not my fault he's still alive and it's not my fault he's still hanging around. I nearly killed Bensen by poisoning his food. None of that was part of our deal. None of it."

"Yeah," Cavanaugh said, mockingly. "*Nearly.* Well, nearly doesn't cut it, Fouser. The governor is looking into this case and my boss can't have that. The stakes are too goddam high. Now, are you going to do what needs to be done here?"

"Like what?" Fouser pleaded. "What do you want me to do? There's only so much . . ."

"Listen," Cavanaugh said. "One call from . . . one call, and you're in a cell instead of taking care of your daughter. The Garrett Bensen case cannot be reopened, for any reason. You need to get a handle on Kaminsky and either get him to back off once and for all or take him out of the picture entirely. If you can't do that, maybe you take another run at Bensen. Either way, this train cannot get off the track. Bensen's case cannot be reopened! Do you understand what I'm telling you?"

Fouser nodded, but no one was in the stairwell to see. He steeled himself.

"Yeah, I do, Mr. Cavanaugh," Fouser said. "But I'm not comfortable with any of this anymore. You and your senator keep your blood money. You do whatever you have to do. Effective immediately, this relationship is over. And you remember, I got cards to play too." He hung up.

"Fouser? Fouser? Goddammit!"

Tommy Cavanaugh stared at the dead phone in his hand before hurling it against the wall of his office.

. . .

Bobby was on the road to the penitentiary when Jim Warren called with the news that someone from Harrisburg was coming to interview Garrett.

"I don't know who and I don't know why, but this is highly unusual," he said.

"I'm heading down anyway," Bobby told him. "How's Garrett doing?"

Bensen was better and was looking forward to getting together.

"He doesn't know about the other meeting yet You may or may not have a chance to talk to him today."

"Care to speculate?"

"Speculation is worthless," Warren said. A buzzer sounded. "Hang on a second."

Bobby heard noise coming from the warden's intercom but couldn't make out what was being said. The only thing he heard clearly from Jim Warren was a loud, "WHO?" He came back on the line.

"Well, things just got interesting," he said. "Your boy is meeting with Weldon Pepper, chief of staff for Governor Tom Hill."

Bobby's eyes glazed over for a moment. "Okay."

"See you when you get here, Mr. Kaminsky. What

is it the Chinese say? It appears that we are living in interesting times."

After hanging up with Warren, Bobby called Al McCarthy to get his take on what this visit from Weldon Pepper might mean.

"They asked if I wanted to sit in on the interview," McCarthy said. "I'm waiting for an x-ray at St. Clair's." Preempting Bobby's question, he added, "Nothing special, just another look at my spine to see if anything has shifted. They take one every six months."

"What do you think this is about?" Bobby asked.

"I don't have to think," he said. "I'm surprised you don't already know." He told Bobby about the email Charlotte Tisdale sent the governor, Micah Previn's short piece in the Harrisburg paper asking the public for help locating a possible witness to the murders of Tisdale, Sheffield, and DiStefano, and the emergence of a new witness, which was potentially explosive.

"So," Bobby began.

"So," McCarthy said. "Mr. Bensen might be getting a stay, whether he wants one or not. Maybe more. Depends on if the governor likes what his chief of staff brings back to the capitol. How you like them apples?"

Bobby laughed. "I like those apples a lot. I'm on my way there now," he told McCarthy. "I'll call you later. Hope you get positive news from the x-ray." Bobby disconnected the call.

He hung up. "Yep," he said aloud. "Those are some excellent fucking apples."

. . .

Jim Warren met Bobby at the gate.

"Things are moving quickly," he said. "Nobody's talked to me, and I haven't talked to Garrett yet. Pepper was in with him for over an hour and on his mobile when he came out. I'm certain he was talking to the governor."

Bobby caught the warden up on his conversations with Drs. Webb and Gable, and with Al McCarthy.

"That's what I've been hearing too," he said. "Speaking personally, I'd rather Bensen pass from his illness than by execution. It never seemed right that this guy should get the needle."

Garrett didn't look well, but he managed a smile when Bobby came in.

"Been an interesting morning, Bobby," he said, almost smiling. "How much of this stuff is you and the other three stooges?"

Bobby put his hands up in mock surrender and shook his head.

"I visited Tisdale's widow down in Sarasota and spoke to a reporter who covered the case," he said. "That's all. But it would be nice if you didn't have an execution date hanging over your head. You know, with your illness and all."

Garrett coughed noisily and took a long pull from a large plastic glass of tea.

"The caffeine actually helps calm my stomach," he said. "Tisdale's widow?" Bobby nodded and laughed.

"You remember Charlotte? The waitress from the Dog?" Bobby asked.

"With the huge tits?" Garrett coughed, sputtering his tea. "She married that shit bag?"

Bobby nodded. Garrett leaned back. "All right, this makes some sense."

"Not too long after I arrived in Darmstadt," Garrett started, reminiscing. "I took a cab into town after a swing. I wanted a beer and a brat, so I went to the Dog. There were a half-dozen people there. Two APs were drinking beer at the table by the door. Another guy and two women were on the other side of the room. I sat down next to the foosball machine. Charlotte moved around the room, taking care of all of us, but eventually she came and sat at my table, probably because I was alone. We talked for a few minutes.

"One of the APs, Tisdale, I guess, called her over.

"'I'll be there in a minute,' she said.

"She turned back to me, and we picked up where we'd left off. He shouted at her again. Real possessive.

"'I told you; I'll be there when I'm finished here,' she said.

"A slow song came on the jukebox. She grabbed my hand. Said, 'Come, *schatzie*. Let's dance.'

"I'm thinking this is my only chance, so we start dancing. She put both arms around my neck and plants this big kiss on my mouth. Halfway through the dance, both APs get up and make a big show, walking out, slamming the front door. Gustav wasn't happy, but I guess he knew not to mess with them.

"Closing time rolled around; I was more than a little tipsy. I asked Charlotte if she wanted me to walk her home, but she said she was fine. Someone would be coming by to pick her up. No mention of who that might be.

"I left, got a little distance between me and the Dog on the way back to the base, when this Jeep pulls up and two guys get out.

"'You got no manners, Bubba,' one of them says to me. It was late, dark. I was wiped. It didn't register who they were. The other said, 'You can drink beer at the Dog, but don't play with the waitress.' He poked me in the chest with his baton. Then the other one grabbed me by my hair and said, 'Watch who you talk to, who you dance with, and definitely watch who you kiss, Bubba.' Then he punched me, first in the gut, then in the face. After that, the two of them just pounded on me. Left me in a heap on the street."

Bobby exhaled. "I remember that night."

"I didn't know who those two assholes were until years later," Garrett said.

"There's a lot happening with your case," Bobby

said. "Apparently, a credible witness has surfaced. I don't know who it is. Charlotte Tisdale, who, by the way, is grateful for what you did, petitioned the governor on your behalf. This very minute, the governor is considering everything from a commutation of your sentence to a full pardon. The Harrisburg newspaper is asking questions about your trial, especially those other crimes the DA tried to bundle into your case."

"You know, Cityboy," he said, "I never understood that," Garrett said. "They had me stone cold on the three I did. I gave them those three, all wrapped up in a bow. How many more times could they kill me? Why did Ianucci add those others into the mix?"

Bobby brought Garrett up to date on Senator Ed Ianucci, how he'd been getting in Bobby's way since he first arrived.

"He's a bad guy, Prettyboy. And he's running for governor. Did you know that?"

Garrett laughed.

"I don't get the news in here, Bobby," he said. "I knew he got elected to the senate, but I didn't know he's running for governor. What does that have to do with me?"

Bobby explained Ianucci was running on a "tough-on-crime" platform, and how Garrett's conviction and eventual execution would burnish the senator's image. But if the conviction was jeopardized, or if Garrett was pardoned, Ianucci's ambitions would be in serious trouble.

"What do you know about the other cases Ianucci added to yours?" Bobby asked.

"Not much," he said. "McCarthy should have that information. Or maybe it's in Jack Parks' case file. He died not too long ago."

"I'll be back," Bobby said. He looked at his old friend. "We're going to get you off death row."

Two guards took Garrett back to his cell. As Bobby exited the interview room another guard approached him.

"Mr. Kaminsky?" he asked.

"That's me," Bobby said. "Fouser, right?"

"Yeah," Fouser said. "Can I walk you outside? I got some things I need to get off my chest."

Chapter 16

obby was almost asleep when his phone rang at eleven that night. He'd just climbed into bed in his room at the Hyatt Regency near the Pittsburgh airport.

"Did I disturb your beauty sleep?" Johnny Lee asked, laughing.

"No," Bobby said. "I'm just sitting here in my hotel room, enjoying an ice-cold glass of delicious, pasteurized, homogenized, Vitamin D–enriched milk."

"As well you should," Farmboy said. "Listen, I need to ask you a question."

"Fire away."

"What was that infection you told me Prettyboy had? The one with his liver?" he asked.

"Hepatitis C," Bobby said. "Nasty stuff. Even with treatment, it can lead to the liver shutting down. It's a killer unless there's a transplant. Garrett's not a candidate because, you know, death row."

Farmboy covered the mouthpiece. The sound was

muffled, but Bobby heard him repeat to someone else the nature of the infection. The other person started a long, drawn-out response, but he couldn't hear it.

"That's what I thought," Farmboy said. "You remember my oldest, John Junior? He graduated Duke some years back. He's got a friend who teaches at the medical school—one of the best in the country."

"I'm not surprised, Johnny," he said. "Duke's a really good school, except maybe in football."

"Okay, now, you watch your mouth," Farmboy said. "Blue Devils gonna do just fine this year. But forget all that. I didn't call you about that."

"What's on your mind?" Bobby asked. "Or, better, what's on John Junior's mind?" Bobby heard the click of the speakerphone.

"Hey, Mr. Kaminsky." His voice sounded just like his father's, but with the vocabulary that comes from a Duke education.

"Nice to talk to someone who speaks English, son," Bobby said. He and his father laughed.

"There's a clinical trial going on in the medical school at Duke and a few other top-tier schools—Emory, Vanderbilt, maybe Stanford," John Junior said. "They're testing a new protocol specifically designed to treat the Hep C virus. I don't know details, but if your and dad's friend gets out of prison—I can't speak for the other schools, but we have a whole boxcar full of connections in Durham. What I'm saying is, he'd have a better-than-average chance of getting in."

Farmboy joined in the conversation. "We are only a hop, skip, and jump from Durham," he said. "Prettyboy gets out, we'll get him into that trial. And we can keep an eye on him too."

Bobby couldn't stop smiling. "That's outstanding," he said. "Let's not get too excited just yet. I'll let Prettyboy know there's an option available to him if things work out."

"He'll have all the milk he wants," Johnny said. "You tell him that."

Bobby had no idea how Prettyboy was sleeping. But after Fouser's *mea culpa* and Farmboy's Duke connections, Cityboy Bobby Kaminsky slept that night like a worn out four-year-old.

• • •

Bobby spent a chunk of his morning on the phone with Micah Previn. They pored over the three unsolved murders Ed Ianucci tried and failed to bundle into Garrett Bensen's prosecution. The cases involved a sex worker, a drug dealer, and a woman with no criminal record who worked in the Dauphin County Elections office. Dauphin County includes the city of Harrisburg; the Dauphin County District Attorney's office is the agency that prosecuted Garrett Bensen's case, and the man who later took charge of the office, the same man who personally prosecuted Garrett, was current Pennsylvania State Senator Eduard Ianucci.

Previn scanned and emailed the case files to Bobby.

Garrett was in Harrisburg during the time of all three homicides. But it was clear no investigative work was performed on any of them. Not entirely surprisingly, Cletus Tisdale caught all three of these cases, ran down a few leads on the prostitute's and dealer's killings, and made sure those two were stamped as unsolved after forty-five days.

The case involving the county employee went cold after twenty-eight days. Except for only the most cursory investigation, the file on the murder of Evelyn Marchesano was light, worth less than nothing in terms of relevant information.

Bobby called Micah again.

"So, how do you read these case files, Micah?"

The reporter didn't hesitate.

"Bull shit, horse shit, dog shit, in that order," Micah said. "The file on Kathy Bensen is missing, and the sex worker, Misty Callahan, was employed by DiStefano at the time of her death."

"What about Mr. Showalter, the drug dealer with a plethora of priors?" Bobby asked.

"He's moderately interesting. A month before his unexpected demise, a high-profile case against him was thrown out because of a blatantly illegal search and seizure. The search produced a weapon, four kilos of cocaine, and nearly eighty thousand dollars in cash, all of which went missing from the county's evidence locker. Wanna take a shot at who conducted the illegal search?"

"Does his name begin with Cletus?"

"Damn! You are good. Thought I'd be able to slip one by you," he said. "The corruption was so rampant, ran so deep, and included so many players," Micah said. "It's amazing the judge had the stones to throw out the case."

"Yeah, well, he didn't throw out Bensen's case," Bobby said. "It looks like his case was also polluted—despite the confession—based on the three dead ends Ianucci tried to sneak in."

"You can't lose sight of the fact Bensen confessed to killing Tisdale, Sheffield, and DiStefano," Micah said. "Say what you will, but Ed Ianucci is a highly skilled prosecutor. With that confession sitting the table . . . it's not surprising."

Bobby and Micah reviewed the files and arrived at the same conclusion. In the cases of the prostitute and the dealer, nothing was there that could help Garrett's cause.

"I'm going to dive deeper into Marchesano," Micah said, "for no other reason than this was the murder of a citizen, a young woman who worked in county government, in the same building as Ianucci and the rest of the DA's office, and there's just nothing substantial in the file. There should have been a whole lot more work put into finding her killer before allowing the case to officially go cold. Now, you've got what I've got. You know what a case file should contain. And this case file doesn't contain any of it."

Bobby opened the file on Evelyn Marchesano.

"A thirty-two-year-old woman is shot and killed in her own home while her husband is on a business trip to Atlanta," Bobby said, reading from Tisdale's notes. "There's no evidence the husband hired the job out, nothing reported stolen, no weapon, no forced entry. There's nothing that implicates anyone. Just a dead body and a clean scene."

"So why would a smart, ambitious guy like Ed Ianucci try to force this case into Garrett Bensen's filing?" Micah asked.

"Why indeed?" Bobby asked. "Now I'm just blue skying a bit here, but from this puny file, the killing of Evelyn Marchesano looks for all intents and purposes like a perfect crime."

"And what do we both know about perfect crimes?"

"Yep," they both said simultaneously.

"There aren't any," said Micah.

"See you soon, Micah." Bobby rang off.

Bobby checked in with Jim Warren before canceling his flight home to Naples. He called Lindy, gave her an apology and an update, and headed straight for Harrisburg.

• • •

One good thing about being a published author with a few successful titles and a film under his belt is that people sometimes want to just chat for a few minutes.

Bobby wasn't worried about Micah; he already had Bobby inked in for dinner that evening. Bobby hoped he could talk to Weldon Pepper, or better, Governor Hill, and not get thrown out on his ass when he arrived unannounced at Ianucci's office. Garrett's execution was scheduled at midnight in eleven days.

"His health seems okay," Warren said. "According to Dr. Gable, the infection could flare up without warning."

Bobby told him the mischief he had in mind for Harrisburg.

"For an English major," Warren said, "you have a pretty large set of balls. Gonna just waltz into Ianucci's office, are you?"

"Waltz? Never. Tango? Maybe. I believe he's just arrogant enough to think he can steamroll me," Bobby said. "I want to push a button or two, see what happens."

Warren wished him luck. Before they ended the call, he dropped the nugget that Dave Fouser, one of Garrett's guards, quit his job earlier that day. No notice.

"He had nearly twenty years in," Warren said. "His daughter has leukemia. He could have pensioned out in nine months. Nine months! Why would he throw that away?"

Bobby was cautious. He chose his words carefully. "I don't think I could say why someone would walk away like that." This wasn't the right moment to enlighten the warden.

"Well, now he's going to wait nearly fifteen years to collect two-thirds of what he would have gotten next year," Warren said. "Maybe he knows something I don't."

Bobby let that dog lie. He told the warden he'd be back in a couple of days and to send his best to Garrett.

Chapter 17

Johnny Lee reached out to Densmore and Allebaugh regarding his son's plan to get Garrett into a clinical trial if he got out of prison. Fatboy called Cityboy.

"Do you think Farmboy knows the difference between a clinical drug trial and a murder trial?" he asked. Allebaugh had a few contacts at Stanford. If things didn't work out at Duke, he'd get into the game.

A glimmer of light shone at the end of this tunnel for Prettyboy. But he was still a triple murderer with a nasty liver infection that didn't care whether he lived or died. Then came an unexpected and most welcome phone call from Charlotte Tisdale.

"You know, Bob," Charlotte said, "I had put my life with Cletus behind me until your visit. Now, I don't know what this is, but while we lived in Harrisburg, Cletus kept a box in our garage labeled *INSURANCE*. I brought it to Florida with me. I thought it might be actual insurance of some kind. Then, in all the confusion following the murder, and then moving, I forgot about it. Just this morning I found it again underneath my potting bench and started looking through it to see if he had a policy I didn't know about. I found file folders with notes, photographs, old cassette tapes. There are a lot of things I don't understand."

"Can you give me an example?" Bobby asked. "I'm on my way to Harrisburg right now so I have time to talk."

He heard her turning pages of paper, muttering to herself.

"What is this?"

"What is what, Charlotte? Just read something to me."

"Well," she said, "Here's something in a file named Winkler. It says, 'Tommy C. said Ed wants Winkler gone.' There's a date—June 12, 1988—and an address: 2211 East Carmel Drive, Elizabethville. There's a picture of . . . oh my God."

"Charlotte?" he said. "What's wrong?"

"There's a picture of a man and then another man—I think it's the same man. In the second picture, he's dead," she said. "My God, what did that horrible man do?" Bobby was pretty sure she wasn't talking about Mr. Winkler.

"I'm going to be at the Hilton in Harrisburg for the next few days. Could you overnight those files to me? I'll reimburse you for everything."

"There's something here with the name Bensen," she said.

He tried to pull over but was stuck in the left lane.

"What does it say?" he asked. "No, never mind. Please just pack it all up and overnight it to me at the Hilton."

"I'll do it right now. You know, Bob, I wrote an email, a long email, to the Pennsylvania governor just like you said."

Bobby smiled. "I do know, Charlotte, and I have to tell you, it has made all the difference in the world. You should be proud."

"I'd be proud if I didn't have to carry Cletus's name with me the rest of my life."

"You don't have to do that. I know someone who owes you a large debt. He'll help you with that after this is all over," Bobby said.

"Someone owes *me* a favor?"

"You have no idea," Bobby said. "You single-handedly changed his life for the better."

• • •

Bobby followed the GPS directions into Harrisburg. He parked, checked in at the front desk of the Hilton downtown, and reached out to Micah Previn. The reporter suggested a small Asian-fusion restaurant near the capitol complex. Bobby took a shower and changed clothes.

They met at 6:30 p.m. Micah took the menu from Bobby's hands and instructed him to let the waiter decide what they'd be eating.

"Everything's great here," he said. "It's good to see you, Bob. You know, without you, none of this happens."

"Nothing's really happened yet, Micah, but some big wheels are turning," Bobby said. "I just hope they're turning in the right direction."

Bobby told him about his chat with Charlotte and the package she'd be sending.

"If any of those three cases are in those files," Micah said. "As Ricky Ricardo said, Ianucci is going to have some 'splainin' to do!"

Bobby asked if the name Winkler rang bells. "Someone from Elizabeth somewhere or other?"

"Elizabethville," Micah said. "It's just north of town. Winkler? No, not off the top of my head, but I didn't work that part of the county. I'll check it out."

They enjoyed a delicious meal. Bobby told him about the book he was writing.

"Let me know if you need anything on my end," Micah offered. "I'm not a book guy; I need to finish what I start before I get up from the keyboard. But once the dust settles, at least where Ianucci and these shit bags are concerned, I'll send whatever I drum up."

Before they parted company for the night, Bobby asked for Micah's take on his plan to pop in on Ed Ianucci.

"The senator has tried to knock me off my game several times since my first trip to SCI-Greene. He had a corrections guard reporting everything back to him. He also used aggressive intimidation tactics on me and Garrett."

"You know this how?" Micah asked.

"I know this because the guard confessed to me before resigning and screwing himself out of his own pension," Bobby said. "He's got some legal problems ahead of him. He told me Ianucci's guy told him to do whatever it took to derail anything that might get Bensen's case reopened, never mind get Garrett out of prison."

"That ship has sailed," Micah said. "Unless Ianucci gets physical again, he is no match for Governor Hill or Weldon Pepper. You may not know it, Bob, but you have some powerful political allies on your side."

"Do you know anything about Ianucci's dirty hands—Cavanaugh?" Bobby asked.

"He's a real sleaze. Did he take a run at you?"

Bobby smiled and nodded. "Yep," he said. "We've met, and I think I may have also enjoyed the pleasure of a visit or two or three by a couple of his middle management team."

Micah picked up the check. Bobby told him he had him on speed dial.

"I'll update you tomorrow." Bobby said.

"I'll get back to you on Winkler."

• • •

Bobby slept late. He left a message for Weldon Pepper, ate breakfast at the Hilton, and alerted the front desk to be on the lookout for a package from Florida. He took a walk toward the capitol building on Commonwealth Avenue. It was a gorgeous day to confront someone.

He thought about calling ahead. It was possible he wouldn't get through security. But that turned out to not be a problem. At the security desk, a uniformed officer asked his name.

"Bob Kaminski. Here to see Senator Ianucci."

The officer made a call. After a few seconds, he handed over a visitor's badge and waved Bobby through.

"Senator Ianucci is expecting you," the guard said.

Bobby knew many politicians were typically full of themselves. They had to be. Why else would they put themselves through an intrusive gauntlet of public scrutiny at such a high level? Part of the reason media exists is to knock self-important, ambitious, influential, or famous people off their pedestals. Ed Ianucci was all four of those things.

But he wasn't always.

• • •

Eduard Antonio Ianucci was the great-grandson of Italian immigrants who arrived in America near the end of the nineteenth century. They settled on the west side of Manhattan until Ed's grandfather, Antonio Ianucci, relocated the family to central Pennsylvania just after the end of WWII. Antonio's son, Tony Ianucci, worked in construction. Ed's mother, Connie, took in laundry and babysat kids in the neighborhood and, in later years, worked as a home health aide.

Young Eduard grew up like a weed, a street kid until his last year in high school, when he managed to pull his academic act together. With the help of good SAT scores and some friends of his father's, Ed earned enough in scholarships to afford Penn State.

He was awarded an undergraduate degree in history, aced the LSAT, and went to law school at Duquesne University in Pittsburgh.

While at Duquesne, Ed had a few inconsequential brushes with the law; a couple of speeding tickets and a resisting arrest charge following an argument with a state trooper. He spent an eventful night in the Allegheny County jail. That one night informed the direction his legal career would take, as well as some notions of his own destiny.

In a surprisingly candid interview Bobby discovered, Ed Ianucci shared what amounted to a revelatory personal experience with a friendly *Philadelphia Enquirer* reporter.

While waiting in a crowded holding cell for the process to play out, Ed was hazed by the other, more experienced prisoners. He was denied access to the one toilet in the cell by a couple of members of a western Pennsylvania motorcycle gang who were coming down from a crystal meth experience. A guy the size of an old oak tree didn't like the way Ianucci looked at him and beat him, badly. All of this occurred in full view of guards who couldn't care less about what happened to some entitled law school brat. Ultimately, the charges against him were dropped, but Ed Ianucci returned to school with a new purpose.

He would never feel powerless like that again. He would never let anyone intimidate him or stop him from achieving his goals, no matter what he had to do.

He was never motivated by money; it was a means to an end, a tool to be used in pursuit of his goals and ambitions. Instead of aiming for a job with a high-dollar firm, after passing the Pennsylvania state bar exam, he signed on as an associate prosecutor with the Dauphin County District Attorney's office. He understood both the power and the opportunities it afforded him. He zealously prosecuted cases he knew he would win and either pleaded out or avoided those with doubtful outcomes. He didn't let technicalities like constitutional due process get in the way of obtaining convictions. He was Machiavellian, using whatever means necessary to achieve the desired outcome, including what he once told Tommy Cavanaugh were "the permanent removal of any and all obstacles to the achievement of success."

Ten years with the Dauphin County DA, after he'd learned to navigate the politics of the office, he ran against the boss and easily won the election for district attorney before his thirty-seventh birthday.

It was the Garrett Bensen case that vaulted the young prosecutor into the state senate, which put Ed Ianucci one step closer to his ultimate goal.

• • •

"Mr. Kaminsky," Ed said, smiling broadly as Bobby walked in. "It's nice to finally meet you. I'm a fan of your work!"

Tom Cavanaugh, wearing a blue striped shirt and paisley tie, stood at Ianucci's right. He smiled more than the occasion merited. "This is Tom Cavanaugh, my senior legislative aide. I think you two might have already met."

Ianucci was a few inches shorter than Bobby, clean-shaven, with slicked-back black hair, dark brown eyes, and a dry olive complexion. He was dressed in a shiny dark-gray sharkskin suit, a white oxford shirt, and a red-and-blue striped tie. His wingtip shoes were shined to a mirror-like gloss.

"Senator," Bobby said, reaching for his outstretched hand. "It's good of you to see me without an appointment." An extra firm handshake, a single nod, and some direct eye contact with Cavanaugh let Ianucci's lackey know that Bobby knew who was behind that parking lot incident in Waynesburg. That ended the show for the benefit of the rest of the staff. Ianucci followed Bobby into his office and closed the door.

"Take a seat," he said.

Bobby sat in one of two red leather chairs in front of an ornate, and only moderately cluttered desk. Had Ianucci removed his jacket and planted himself in the other chair, Bobby might have believed the visit would be collegial, if not warm. Instead, he stayed standing with his jacket still on. He placed his hands on his desk blotter and leaned in.

"What the fuck do you think you're doing, Kaminsky?"

Bobby stood, looked down at the desk, placed his own hands on either side of a wooden, hand-carved *Senator Eduard Ianucci* desk sign, and leaned in himself, their faces only inches apart.

"Senator, I'm here for only one reason, and that is to encourage you, in the interests of justice, to take the lead role in reopening the case against Garrett Bensen. It's the right thing," he said, pointing at him. "And you'll be a hero with Pennsylvanians who don't share your enthusiasm for the death penalty."

Ianucci removed his jacket and placed it on a hook attached to the back of his office door. He sat down in his own chair, folded his hands across his midsection, and leaned back.

"And why would I do that? Garrett Bensen confessed. A jury of his peers convicted him. He was sentenced in accordance with commonwealth guidelines. He's going to die soon. In the end, all your shenanigans will amount to nothing. And by the way, Pennsylvania voters do support capital punishment—by an impressive margin."

Shenanigans, Bobby thought. *I'll show you shenanigans.*

"Do you know the name Winkler? I believe he was from Elizabethville?"

Ianucci would be eaten alive in a poker game. His face went slack.

"Winkler? Where the fuck did that come from?"

Bobby sat down. "Not entirely sure yet, but I will be. Probably before the sun sets today. What about Evelyn Marchesano? Remember her?"

Ianucci stood straight. He took in and then let out a deep breath. He stabbed Bobby with ice-cold eyes.

"I don't know what you think you know or what you think you're doing, Kaminsky, but you can get the fuck out of my office and get the hell out of my state."

Robert L. Kaminski morphed into Bobby K. from Sheepshead Bay. He took a step forward.

"Just so we're clear, Senator, unlike some others around here, you don't scare me at all. I've already handled some of the best shots you're going to take at me. I know how hard you've tried to scare me off, to hurt me. But I'm just getting started. The research for my book on the Bensen case has some interesting sludge bubbling to the surface. And it's full of your filthy fingerprints."

Ianucci started to come at him. Bobby walked out,

slamming the door behind him. He crashed into Tom Cavanaugh, who landed flat on his ass on the carpeted floor.

"Sorry, Tom," Bobby said, helping him up. "Your boss may need a cup of chamomile, and you may want to take a minute to evaluate this working relationship of yours. It may not be too late to save yourself. There's some real ugliness coming his way." Bobby exited Ianucci's office suite.

The senator slumped into his chair. A single name repeated in his mind: Evelyn Marchesano.

• • •

September 1991

The bedside telephone rang once in the master suite of the two-story house in Colonial Park occupied by Cletus and Charlotte Tisdale, and their young daughter, Christa.

"Yeah?" Tisdale mumbled.

"Wake the fuck up!" Tisdale recognized the voice immediately—Assistant District Attorney Ed Ianucci.

"I'm awake," he said.

"I need you to do something and I need it done right now!"

Shit, Cletus thought, looking at the clock by the side of the bed. His wife turned over.

"What time is it?" she asked.

"It's the middle of the damn night," he said. "Go back to sleep."

"What did you say?" Ianucci asked.

"I wasn't talking to you, sir," he said. "The phone woke up my wife."

"Meet me at the Hillcrest Diner in thirty minutes. It's on—"

"I know where it is," he snapped. "I'm a damn HPB sergeant, in case you forgot." There was silence at the other end. Shit, the cop thought, man must be up against a big-ass wall this time.

"You need to remember who you're talking to, Sergeant," Ianucci said. "And you need to remember what I know and what I can do with what I know. Now get up, get dressed, and get moving." He paused. "And wear your uniform!"

Sergeant Tisdale dressed and tied his shoes.

"Where are you going?" his wife asked.

"You don't need to worry about that," he said. "Go back to sleep." He slipped quietly through the bedroom door, down the stairs, and out of the house.

• • •

The two men sat silently across from one another staring at cups of coffee. There was an oversized blueberry muffin in front of the cop.

"Let me get this straight, . . ." the cop began.

"Shut your fucking mouth," Ianucci whispered. "You

heard me. You know what needs to be done. I am not fucking around with you." He handed Tisdale a folded piece of paper. "The deed is already done. All you have to do is clean the scene. Make everything go away. All you need to know is right there."

The cop studied the paper. He sighed heavily. Tisdale knew what his role was. And he knew this was personal.

"This ain't right, man," he said. "I know the drill, Bubba, but this just plain ain't right."

The waitress brought the check. "You two be careful out there," she said.

The cop moved his bulky body out of the booth and strode to his cruiser. "Just ain't fucking right," he muttered.

No, Ianucci thought, *it isn't. But it is what it is.* He watched Tisdale sit in his cruiser for a good five minutes, then drive off. He finished his coffee, left a ten for the waitress, and walked to his car.

• • •

Tisdale arrived at 4:17 a.m. at the address Ianucci had given him. The front door was closed but unlocked. He walked inside, using his flashlight to find his way. If anyone wondered about his being there, he'd say he received a tip from a "confidential informant" who saw someone running from the house. He wasn't worried. There'd be no questions.

Evelyn Marchesano's body was exactly where Ianucci told him it would be. To Tisdale's trained eyes, she'd been strangled and left where she landed. Unfortunately, she'd landed on her nose and bled onto the cream-colored carpeting in the living room. Even with more time, Tisdale wasn't sure he could get rid of the body, get rid of the bloodstain in the carpet, and wipe off the fingerprints. *At least*, Tisdale thought, *it was her blood and not Ianucci's.*

The cop knew he was alone on this; Artie and Joey couldn't be trusted to help clean up Ianucci's affair. He snapped on latex gloves and methodically moved from room to room, wiping down every object he saw. When he finished, he drove to a pay telephone outside a convenience store. He dialed 911.

"Nine-one-one. What's your emergency?"

"I think something bad happened at my neighbor's house," he said, talking as fast as he could. He spoke the address and hung up the phone before the operator could ask more questions.

He drove to a gas station and called Ianucci.

"Who is this?" Ianucci asked. Tisdale ignored the question.

"Any forensic evidence at the house has been eliminated. There was blood—her blood—on the carpet so the scene couldn't be cleaned. I'll handle things in the morning." He didn't wait for an answer. He hung up, got into his car, and drove home.

•••

Almost a year later, in August 1992, Tommy Cavanaugh entered Ianucci's office without his customary two knocks.

"You heard?"

"Heard what?" the ADA asked.

"It's not good," he said. "I'm glad you're sitting down."

"What do I need to be sitting down for?"

Cavanaugh put his mug of coffee onto a coaster next to the wood-carved nameplate on the desk.

"Spit it out, Tommy," Ianucci said. "I don't have time for bullshit."

Cavanaugh looked away. He hated this. He'd known Ed Ianucci since law school. He was the kind to take his anger out on the messenger.

"Tommy, do me a favor, okay? Get the fuck out of my office until you grow a pair of—"

"There was a triple murder downtown last night," Cavanaugh said.

"And?" Ianucci said.

"And the victims are three men who are very well known to us and with whom we have had a mutually advantageous connection."

Ianucci leaned back. He stared into his classmate's eyes. "Say it!"

"Cletus Tisdale, Arthur Sheffield, and Joseph DiStefano. Somebody killed all three of them in an alley downtown. Maybe try, every now and then, to not be such a fucking asshole. Especially to the people close to you." Tommy Cavanaugh stood up, grabbed his mug of coffee, and left his boss to consider the ramifications of their situation.

Ianucci processed the information and jogged the thirty feet to his boss's office. He knocked twice and walked in. The district attorney of Dauphin County looked up from his work.

"What do you need?" he asked.

"I heard there was some excitement downtown last night," Ianucci said. "I want this one."

. . .

September 2016

"Tommy!" Ianucci called. "Now!"

Tom Cavanaugh walked into his boss's office and closed the door. Ianucci sat quietly. The senator broke the staring contest.

"I want eyes on that motherfucker from now until he's either dead or gone," Ianucci said. "You have him watched, and if the situation presents itself, I want him dead *and* gone."

"Sir, I think—"

Ianucci's eyes went from alive and on fire to completely dead.

"I've told you, Tommy, way too many times. It's my

job to think. It's your job to do exactly what the fuck I tell you to do. You understand what's at stake?"

Tom Cavanaugh nodded his head.

"No more screw-ups or excuses. This asshole is disrupting the most important moment in my life, and therefore your life, Tommy," Ianucci said, as if talking to a small child. "Now, one last time, do you understand what I need from you?"

"Yes, sir," Cavanaugh said. He left the senator to smolder in silence.

• • •

Bobby checked his phone and saw he'd missed a return call from Weldon Pepper. He listened to the voice mail. They'd meet in an unmarked office in the south wing of the same building at 1:15 p.m.

On the short walk back to the hotel, Bill Densmore called.

"What are you up to, Cityboy?" he asked.

"Just disturbing the shit," Bobby said. "Stirring the pot." Bobby filled him in on his chat with Charlotte the day before, his dinner with Micah, and his three minutes with Ed Ianucci.

"Wow! Sorry I'm missing all the fun," he said. "I spoke to Don Sittler. He's the Pennsylvania Supreme Court justice I went to law school with up in Boulder. He's inclined to extend the court's earlier stay indefinitely, depending on the nature and amount of evidence he can cite in his opinion."

"Hopefully I'll have Charlotte's package this afternoon," Bobby said. "It won't take much to link one or more of the additional cases Ianucci tried to bundle in with Prettyboy's back to the senator from Harrisburg. I'm scheduled to meet with the governor's chief of staff at 1:15. Let's catch up after that."

Chapter 18

Bobby walked back to the Hilton. His room was being serviced by housekeeping, so he grabbed his messenger bag and took the elevator back to the lobby. There, he opened his laptop and searched for the website of *The Harrisburg Patriot-News*. When the site loaded, a headshot of Micah Previn blared back at him. The headline read, "Award-Winning *Patriot* Reporter Victim of Vicious Assault." Bobby's heart sank.

Micah was on a ventilator at Harrisburg Hospital. He had been attacked minutes after leaving the restaurant where they'd had dinner.

The front desk clerk approached him.

"Mr. Kaminsky?" she asked.

"Uh huh," he said, absently staring at the picture of Micah.

"Two HPB detectives asked to see you, sir." She pointed to where they were standing.

Bobby closed his computer and accompanied her to the front desk. There, he met Detectives Eric Brunner and Ernest Cleaveland of the Harrisburg Police Bureau's Major Crimes Section. They walked to a more private area in the lobby when the same desk clerk came back and heaved a bank box at Bobby. It was from Charlotte Tisdale.

"Your package from Florida, sir." He thanked her and sat down with the two detectives.

"Is this about Micah? I just saw it on *The Patriot* website," he said.

"It is," said Brunner. "You were with him last night?"

"I was. We had dinner at an Asian place."

"Tokyo Sunset," he said. "We found the receipt in his pocket, along with your name, the name of this hotel, and some other scribbles. We're hoping you can fill some holes for us."

"What happened to him?" Bobby asked.

"Best we can tell right now, he was ambushed near his car, about a block and a half from Tokyo Sunset," Detective Cleaveland said. "Can you tell us the nature of your business with Mr. Previn?"

Bobby put both his hands on the sides of his head.

"I met him last night for the first time. We've only known each other over the phone, until yesterday," he said. "I'm here researching a book about an old friend who's on death row over at Waynesburg."

"Garrett Bensen," Cleaveland said. It wasn't a question.

"Yes, Detective. Garrett and I served together in the air force in the '80s," Bobby said.

"Eric," Cleaveland said to his partner. "Would you give me and Mr. Kaminsky a minute, please?"

"Sure." Brunner nodded, excused himself, and walked toward the large coffee urn the Hilton kept available for guests.

"Mr. Kaminsky," Cleaveland said, "I've known Micah Previn for some time. He's a good guy, a solid reporter, and he doesn't make enemies. He's working some new information on the Bensen case. He revealed recently there might have been a witness to the murders Bensen committed and confessed to."

"That's right," Bobby said. "He covered the original trial. That's how I discovered him. Is he going to be all right?"

"No way to know right now," he said. "They're calling his condition 'guarded.' Mr. Kaminsky, I witnessed those murders when I was a fifteen-year-old kid who literally happened to be in the wrong place at the wrong time. I don't believe in coincidences; I think Micah's attack is related to the Bensen case. Do you have any thoughts on who might have done this to him?"

Bobby stared at the apparition in front of him. A witness. *The* witness. And a Harrisburg Police detective to boot!

"I need to open this box I just received, Detective Cleaveland. There might be some answers inside."

Bobby had an hour before his meeting with Weldon Pepper. He opened the FedEx box and found several thick envelopes filled with multicolored file folders. Each folder had a name on it. Most had audiocassette tapes inside. Winkler's file was on top. The Bensen file was next. He opened it and started scanning the first page.

Tommy C. said Ed would bury Bensen woman case. Ed helped with Bensen woman. AS and JD now work for Ed and Tommy C.

Bobby was looking at the original police file on Kathy Cobb-Bensen's murder. The note was attached with a paper clip.

Bobby scanned a few of the other folders. Many he didn't recognize. Then he came across Callahan and Showalter. He went further and found a file with the name Marchesano.

Ed personally did Evelyn M. I handled scene cleanup. Learned later from Tommy C. they were an item. Ed worried what she might say or do. Strangled her.

Bobby put the Bensen file back in the box and handed the Callahan, Marchesano, and Showalter files to Detective Cleaveland.

"I'm not the expert here, Detective, but it looks like Ed Ianucci was using Tisdale, Sheffield, and DiStefano as his own personal dirty deeds squad," Bobby said. "He swept the murder of Bensen's wife under the rug for Tisdale and the others, which indebted them to him. When he needed someone worked over or a crime scene cleaned, like Marchesano, one or more of these three did the work.”

“Where in God’s name did you come up with this?” Cleaveland asked. Bobby showed him the return label on the FedEx box. The detective’s eyes narrowed.

“Long story, Detective. Some other time.”

“I need to show this to my captain.”

Bobby wasn’t ready to let the box of evidence out of his hands.

“I want to check in on Micah, then I have a meeting with Weldon Pepper,” he said. “Soon as I finish, how about you and I and this box go visit your boss together?”

The detective looked Bobby right in the eyes. After a moment, he nodded.

“Tell you what, my partner and I will come with you to the hospital,” Detective Cleaveland said. “Then we’ll take you to the capitol for your meeting with Mr. Pepper. Then we’ll visit with my people. That work for you?” Bobby stood up, closed the bank box, and all three left through the front door of the hotel.

• • •

Micah Previn was in the ICU on a ventilator, a guard stationed at his door. Cleaveland got Bobby into the room, but it was doubtful they’d be able to talk. Micah had been beaten, badly. *Why*, Bobby wondered to himself, *would anyone with even half a brain risk beating up a reporter?* Considering the incident in the Outback parking lot and the shooting on the interstate, Bobby guessed these thugs weren't exactly top-tier muscle. *They made a mistake*, Cityboy thought. *The beating was meant for him.*

He stayed as long as he could, but he didn't want to miss his meeting with Weldon Pepper. Before leaving, he leaned down and whispered to the unresponsive reporter all the news he could before an officious nurse moved him along.

"How long before Micah will be awake?" Bobby asked her.

"Are you family?"

"Close friend."

"For you, it will be a while," she said, and then she pointed to Cleaveland and Brunner. "These gentlemen have questions. Then family, if there is any. After that, we'll see."

"When do you think the police will be able to ask their questions?" Bobby asked.

"Maybe early evening. It's a guess."

• • •

Bobby climbed into the back seat of the detectives' car. Brunner drove.

"So," Cleaveland began, "where did you get those files?"

Cityboy wanted no space between himself and the Harrisburg Police Bureau. "A few days ago, I met with Cletus Tisdale's ex-wife. Yesterday, she called me to report finding this box in her garage. She had no idea he'd kept these notes. The original box was marked *INSURANCE*. It's not a stretch to believe he kept these notes in case his arrangement with Iannucci and Tommy Cavanaugh went sour."

Cleaveland nodded. "What's your stake in all this?"

"I knew Garrett Bensen," Bobby said. "When I learned what he did—what he confessed to doing—I had no real choice but to find out what had happened. Now, though, in addition to seeing all of this through, I'm going to tell his story in a book."

"Oh," Brunner said. "You're that Kaminski? The writer?"

"Author," Bobby corrected.

Cleaveland nodded. They pulled into a parking space reserved for the HPB in front of the capitol.

"Maybe," Cleaveland said, "when you finish telling the story, you'll let folks know that Harrisburg is a way different city now than it was back then."

"You have my word on that, Detective," Bobby said.

• • •

Weldon Pepper met Bobby at building security. He had a visitor's badge in one hand and shook Bobby's with the other.

"Mr. Kaminsky, you're responsible for upsetting a

number of apple carts here in Harrisburg," he said. "Therefore, I am delighted to meet you."

"You have no idea how surprising all the commotion has been, Mr. Pepper," he said. "Please, call me Bob."

"Weldon," he answered.

They arrived at a small conference room on the third floor. A Pennsylvania State Trooper opened the door and let them in.

"Who called this meeting?" Weldon asked.

"I guess we both did," Bobby said. "You paid a visit to my friend, Garrett Bensen. I recently met your boss's opposition in the next election. I guess we have those things to talk about."

The meeting lasted an hour. Bobby brought Weldon Pepper up to speed with what he'd begun referring to as the Charlotte files. Weldon was angry about what had happened to Micah Previn.

"I have to tell you, Bob," he said, "I know Ianucci's a bully and that he's a holdover from a corrupt criminal justice system that ran roughshod over this beautiful city," Weldon said. "But I never imagined he was capable of this kind of stuff."

He poured glasses of water. Bobby gulped his down.

"Do you have time to get something to eat?" Weldon asked.

"You read my mind," Bobby said. "I'm starving."

They took an elevator to the cafeteria in the basement of the capitol. Bobby got a breaded chicken cutlet with a baked potato and early peas. Weldon opted for the open-face roast beef sandwich, mashed potatoes, and glazed carrots. No money changed hands at the register.

"How do you think this is going to play out?" Bobby asked. "Right now, I'm asking regarding Garrett Bensen."

"I got a call this morning from Donald Sittler," he said.

"The supreme court justice," Bobby said. "He's an old friend of another old friend."

"I can't be certain, of course, not being a part of the Pennsylvania criminal justice system," he said, "but if Bensen's appellate attorney—Albert McCarthy, I believe—happened to petition the Pennsylvania Supreme Court for an indefinite stay of Mr. Bensen's scheduled execution . . . it wouldn't be out of the realm of possibility."

Bobby chuckled at Weldon Pepper's politically safe speech. "I'm sure that can be made to happen," Bobby said.

They wolfed down their lunch. Bobby called Al McCarthy, filled him in on the necessary details, and got the appeal wheel turning.

"I don't know what you do or don't know about this whole affair," Bobby said to Weldon.

"I'm not sure, but I think I know pretty much all there is to know that's relevant to my boss and the citizens of the commonwealth."

Bobby reminded him that Garrett had spent much

of his adult life at SCI-Greene under a death sentence that, under even minimally different circumstances, would never have been imposed.

"In fact, Weldon," he said, "had what I've learned in the past few weeks been known at either his trial, at sentencing, or at any of his appeals, there's an excellent chance Garrett Bensen would already be a free man."

He gave Weldon the status of Garrett's health, and shared his knowledge of the possibility, should he be pardoned anytime soon, he might be able to take advantage of a drug trial, which could leave him with something resembling a future.

The governor's chief of staff hesitated before responding. It was, of course, a good-news, bad-news kind of thing.

"The guy upstairs—I'm talking about Governor Hill, not . . . the other guy upstairs—is, I'm relatively certain, inclined to not oppose a reduction in sentence for Mr. Bensen."

"He's been on death row for twenty-three years. Had the presiding judge and jury been aware of all the mitigating circumstances, he'd already be out."

"That may be true. But he's confessed to murdering three people. One of them a sworn police officer for the city of Harrisburg."

"Whose own wife dances on his grave every chance she gets," Bobby said.

"There are three competing forces at work," Weldon said. "There's the law, there's public perception, and there's politics. The law takes care of itself, or it's supposed to. It's the second and third that the governor must consider before commuting his sentence or possibly even pardoning Garrett Bensen. You and Mrs. Tisdale have provided a great deal of political cover."

"Doesn't hurt that his political rival will be so covered in shit, the stink will never go away," Bobby said. "Sorry, Weldon. Even for me, that was a bit indelicate."

They deposited their trays and plates into a cart near the door and climbed a flight of stairs to the main lobby. Weldon extended his hand.

"I wish I had even one friend as good and committed as you, Bob," he said.

Bobby returned the visitor badge. In politics, if someone wants a friend, they need to get a dog. "You will," Bobby said. "Maybe five-fold if we can pull this off."

. . .

Bobby had an hour-long meeting with Detectives Cleaveland and Brunner, along with a few members of the HPB brass. All of them were blown away by the contents of the files Charlotte Tisdale had provided. When it was decided they'd wait a bit before confronting Senator Iannucci, a tired Cityboy Bobby Kaminsky asked for and received a ride back to the Hilton.

Chapter 19

Bobby tried taking a nap before checking in with the hospital as to Micah Previn's condition. But he couldn't shut off his brain. Instead, he reviewed the last several weeks of his life and studied the notion of friendship.

He recalled a line but couldn't identify the source. Friends come into someone's life for a reason, for a season, or for a lifetime. Bobby was blessed to have had good friends for a season, a long time ago. Since he stumbled across that blurb in *USA Today*, he had reconnected with them. Now he had four friends for life.

He vowed to not take such valuable people lightly ever again, and to never forget the people on the journey with him.

His contemplation was interrupted by a call from Detective Cleaveland. Micah Previn was out of danger and looking forward to seeing him. Bobby splashed cold water on his face and headed to the hospital to visit with yet another, this time newly found, friend.

• • •

Micah sat up in bed. He was a mess, but he managed a small smile for Bobby.

"I know," he said. "I look like I got the shit kicked out of me."

Bobby nodded. "Yep," he said. "Any idea who did this?"

"I got a good look at one of the guys and gave Brunner's sketch artist something to work with," he said. "I'm still a reporter. I'm trained to be observant."

"I'm really sorry, Micah," Bobby said, "but I'm pretty sure the beating you took was meant for me."

Micah laughed, even though it hurt.

"Don't be so self-centered, Mr. Kaminsky," he said. "Reporters are easy targets. We write stuff that pisses people off all the time."

"I guess that's true," Bobby said. He didn't believe it for a second. "Brunner and Cleaveland appear to be good cops."

"They are good," Micah said. "It's a much better department now than it was in the bad old days."

Bobby updated Micah on the contents of Charlotte Tisdale's package, the meeting with Weldon Pepper, and his encounter with Ed Ianucci. They agreed this was the work of Ianucci's henchmen.

"What's next?" Micah asked.

Bobby shrugged. "Maybe I'll take another run at the good senator."

"You are a glutton for punishment," Micah said. "Wish I could go with you." Bobby smiled. He thought for a moment.

"Can you? I mean, if you could get released and if you could physically and emotionally handle it, would you consider walking in there with me, and maybe with a couple of guys with guns and badges who seem like the goods?"

Micah pointed behind Bobby. "Let's ask her." His doctor entered the room.

Micah was released two hours later. After he picked up fresh clothes and toiletries, Bobby got him a room at the Hilton. Even cleaned up, Micah looked like a guy who'd spent too much time in a small cave with a large mountain lion.

• • •

When he called Bobby later that night, Johnny Lee was still leading the charge for Garrett to get into the Hepatitis C drug trial at Duke.

"It's pretty much a done deal," he said. "Helps that we donate a few bucks to Blue Devil nation every year."

"Things may start to happen fast," Bobby said. "So, you may want to make whatever arrangements are necessary. Or have Johnny Junior clear the decks."

"Consider those decks cleared," Johnny said. "Gonna feed that boy a whole lotta North Carolina milk."

Fatboy took the news with slight skepticism.

"You really think he'll get out?" he asked. "I mean,

I'd love to see it. But he killed three people, got a death sentence. It's not like one of those 'some other dude did it' things," he said.

"No, he did it," Bobby said. "But he's done twenty-three years on death row. There were extenuating circumstances that would have impacted his sentence, possibly nullified the jury's verdict."

"Well," he said. "That surprise I'm putting together? It works either way. Report back when you know something."

. . .

Bill Densmore was ahead of things, as usual.

"Glad you called Cityboy. I just got off the phone with Don Sittler," he said. "Soon as he gets a motion, he's prepared to hand down an indefinite stay of execution. Then the ball bounces over to the governor's court. It's up to him as to say whether Prettyboy dies, gets his sentence commuted, or gets pardoned and exits from the hell he's been in."

Bobby told him about Micah, Weldon Pepper, and his meeting with Ed Ianucci.

"I asked Don about the senator," Bill said. "They came up professionally at the same time in Harrisburg. His completely off the record report was that the three words to describe Ed Ianucci are despicable, delusional, and dangerous. It seems Ed Ianucci has a reputation for having stepped over several bodies—metaphorically of course—that were left in his wake as he climbed the ladder in Pennsylvania. He spent his whole career as an ADA rolling over anyone who got in his way. Uses people, then discards them. He's got a huge sense of entitlement. He believes he's on his way to the White House and is launching the third step in his four-step plan."

· · ·

Ed Ianucci always believed deep down that he had an appointment with destiny. When he married Vicki Lamonica, the daughter of central Pennsylvania real estate developer Dominic Lamonica, love had nothing to do with it. It was about timing.

Ed met Vicki at Penn State. He was earning his undergrad in history; she was focused on a business degree. He chose law school at Duquesne in Pittsburgh, while she went east to Philadelphia and obtained a master's in business administration from Wharton. Both would wind up in Harrisburg. Vicki joined her father's construction company, based in southern Dauphin County. Ed took a job as a Dauphin County assistant district attorney.

They were often in the same room at political gatherings and charity events. They started dating. Vicki was shopping for a husband. Ed was shopping for connections that would serve his political ambitions. He was a handsome, young prosecutor and never had to look far for casual companionship.

At her father's urging, Vicki persisted in getting closer to him.

"This guy is going places," her father had told her. "Don't be too patient. He'll be helpful for the business. You could do worse." Vicki worshipped her father and did as he suggested.

Ed knew at some point he'd have to settle down. In his mind, Vicki was good wife material. Shorter than him, nicely put together, whip-smart, and from a well-connected Italian family. Plenty of women were good for fun, but not for the long haul. Ed didn't love Vicki, but he liked her well enough to keep her close.

Ed was twenty-five when he joined the Dauphin County DA's office as an assistant district attorney Three years later, he and Vicki pragmatically decided they'd be better together than for each of them to continue looking for some notion of perfect. Ed had plans; he needed a wife and eventually a family. Vicki was all about her family's business interests; she viewed Ed Ianucci, a successful prosecutor with a future in politics, as an excellent investment.

In 1986, Ed and Vicki got married. It was the main event of the Harrisburg social season. They'd agreed not to burden themselves with children anytime soon—another business arrangement. Vicki's family wanted someone inside the government power structure. Ed wanted access to the money Dominic Lamonica could raise for future campaigns.

Ed essentially lived his life as if he and Vicki were in a convenient partnership. Vicki worked her way up in her father's company. By all outward appearances, they were an attractive power couple. At home, they slept in separate bedrooms.

In early 1991, Ed began a clandestine affair with Evelyn Marchesano, an attractive, married Dauphin County employee. It went on for several months. When she pressed him to divorce Vicki, he lost his well-documented temper and, after a short but passionate shouting match, he strangled her to death in the living room of her home. He had Cletus Tisdale—the HPB cop who'd been in his debt for Ed having buried the murder of Kathy Cobb-Bensen—clean up the scene.

Dominic had encouraged Ed to run for DA following Garrett Bensen's conviction. His colleague, Tom Cavanaugh, ran Ed's campaign while Dominic chaired Ed's finance committee. Ed won a close election to DA in 1996 over the man who'd hired him. He ran unopposed in 2000 and 2004. He could have stayed in the job forever, but both Ed and Dominic were ambitious. Dominic saw a future governor in Ed Ianucci. Ed's vision went even further. In 2008, with Dominic's encouragement and support, Ed ran for the Pennsylvania State Senate and won—handily—after the six-term incumbent retired.

Ed grew consumed with his notion of destiny. In 2012, Tom Hill, formerly mayor of Scranton, ran for governor of Pennsylvania and won. In September of 2015, against Dominic's advice, Ed decided to run against Tom Hill in 2016. Governor Hill was well liked and polled very well; Dominic wanted Ed to wait until 2020. Ed was in a hurry.

When he was elected governor—there were never any *ifs* in Ed's mind—he would be fifty-five. In eight years, he'd be sixty-three, the perfect time for a two-term, swing-state governor to make a run for the White House. He'd retire at seventy-one, after serving two terms, and would write a book and live out his life—powerful, wealthy, and famous.

Ed Ianucci had it all worked out.

In November 2015, disenchanted with Ed's out-of-control ambition and unwillingness to listen to him, Dominic convinced Vicki to file for divorce. Ed didn't miss a beat. He pressed on, without Dominic's support, without children, and without his wife. Women, especially after the Marchesano affair, no longer interested Ed Ianucci. They'd become a distraction. Pursuing power had become his sole passion.

• • •

"I met this guy, Cowboy," Bobby said. "I doubt he'd even be cleared for a tour of the White House." Densmore said he was just reporting what his friend, Pennsylvania Supreme Court Justice Don Sittler, had told him. Bobby couldn't process how someone like Ianucci could have the audacity to put out such a plan and then commit to it so strongly he'd literally kill to get there.

"Your friend said the third word to describe Ianucci was dangerous?"

"I guess this comes under the heading of unsubstantiated rumor, but apparently a woman Ianucci was involved with—a married woman—was murdered under some very suspicious circumstances," Densmore said. "That case was never solved. Plus, and this is definitely in the bizarre column, Don told me that several felons who Ianucci tried but couldn't prosecute wound up dead the within a year after they were exonerated."

Bobby connected the dots as Cowboy laid out what he'd learned. The woman was Evelyn Marchesano. That would explain why so little went into investigating her case. The others were likely garnish killings, designed to keep Tisdale, Sheffield, and DiStephano busy and committed to serving their master. It all ended when Garrett Bensen met them in that alley behind Fourth Street near Peffer in downtown Harrisburg.

Now, Bobby thought, *everything made sense, all of it.*

"According to Don, a local political gadfly tried to get someone to investigate these allegations, but he turned up dead. Also, under mysterious circumstances."

"Yeah," Bobby said, "that was a guy named Winkler. And we know about the others thanks to the Tisdale files."

"All this fits with what you've learned?"

"Fits perfectly," Bobby said. "We're going to bring down this asshole, and we're going to do it using the full force of the justice system now in place for such things."

"Give 'em hell, Cityboy," Densmore said. "Give me a call after it all gets done. And you be careful! Remember, this guy may be delusional, but he also definitely is dangerous."

• • •

Bobby checked out of the Hilton, planning to drive to Waynesburg after they ambushed Ianucci that morning. He and Micah ate breakfast together at the hotel.

"I looked into the Winkler murder," Micah said. "In hindsight, not one of our finest moments at *The Patriot-News*."

"Let me guess," Bobby said. "He knew some bad things went down, tried to get someone to look into it, couldn't, and got himself killed for his trouble."

"You already knew?" Micah asked. Bobby told him about his conversation with Bill Densmore, leaving out the part about the Tisdale files for the moment.

"Didn't you drop Winkler's name with Ianucci yesterday?"

"I did," Bobby said. "I think it rattled him."

"How do you think this morning's adventure will play out?"

Before he could answer, Detectives Brunner and Cleaveland entered the Hilton's lobby. Bobby waved them over.

"You guys need breakfast?" he asked.

"Coffee's fine," said Brunner. They sat down. Cleaveland turned to Micah.

"You provided good information about the creeps who assaulted you," he said, showing Micah a mug shot. "We picked up a Mr. Detlef Grunewald last night. He matches your description."

"Did he give up the others?" Micah asked. Brunner laughed.

"Oh yeah. Took him a matter of seconds," he said. "Mr. Grunewald is twenty-four, fresh off an Amish farm outside Lancaster. Didn't get far enough, I guess. We've got uniforms collecting the others."

"Did Grunewald say why he and his crew worked Micah over?" Bobby asked.

Brunner couldn't keep a straight face.

"He did. He thought it was you they were working over. Got scared this morning when he saw the newspaper."

Bobby gave Micah a sidelong glance.

"Said the order came from Tom Cavanaugh," Cleaveland said. He looked at Micah. "Detlef claims he stopped the others from killing you."

Micah shrugged. "I don't know about that," he said. "Too busy getting the shit kicked out of me. Felt like there were eight of them."

"We'll toss it in Ianucci's direction, see if he reaches for it," Brunner said.

"We have so much going on," Bobby said, ticking off all the evidence involving Evelyn Marchesano, the murders Ianucci bundled into Garrett's case, Mr. Winkler and his story, Charlotte's files, and the coup de grâce, Fouser's full confession followed by an unexpected early retirement.

"Shame that's just hearsay evidence," Cleaveland said.

"I can't believe I'm the one saying this, but maybe he'll go on record if we can get him his pension and keep him out of prison," Bobby said.

"Let me run that up our chain of command and talk to some folks at the PDLE," Cleaveland said. "His formal statement would be icing on this cake. He'd bury Tommy Cavanaugh. I'll bet Cavanaugh's loyalty only goes so far."

Micah and Bobby finished their breakfast. Cleaveland and Brunner finished their coffee. The four of them were headed out when Cleaveland's phone rang.

"I need to take this. You head on over. Eric and I will catch up," he said. "Wait for us in the lobby at the capitol."

Bobby and Micah walked out onto North Second Street. Next stop, the Pennsylvania statehouse and another surprise visit with Senator Ianucci. The sky was blue, the sun was shining, and the temperature was hot, and getting hotter. Bobby entertained the thought that the meeting would be fun.

"We've got Senator Asshole dead to rights," he said.

"Don't underestimate him," Micah said. "He's ruthless on a good day and right now he's cornered."

Bobby nodded absently at what Micah said. He was

distracted by the black SUV making its way up the street. The passenger side window slid down.

"Gun!" Bobby yelled, and shoved Micah to the ground.

There were three quick pops. One of the bullets skimmed Bobby's shoulder before hitting a civilian walking behind him.

Bobby caught Detective Cleaveland out of the corner of his eye. He had his gun aimed at the SUV. He shot twice. One round shattered the windshield of the Honda Pilot and lodged in the driver's right temple. The shooter in the passenger's seat dropped his weapon and put both his hands out the window. Clearly, he'd seen this movie before. The SUV drifted to the right, scraping three cars parked alongside the hotel's entrance before coming to a stop in front of the Hilton's driveway.

"Keep your hands where I can see them," Brunner screamed at the shooter, leveling his own pistol. Micah attended to the pedestrian, who unfortunately, as with Detective Cleaveland decades earlier, had simply been in the wrong place at the wrong time.

"Need some help over here," Micah shouted. Passersby were on their phones, calling for assistance, shooting video. Bobby checked his shoulder to assess the damage.

"EMT's on the way," Cleaveland said to Bobby. "Micah, you okay?"

"I'm fine thanks to Mr. Kaminsky here," Micah said. He pointed at the injured civilian. "This guy needs help."

The pedestrian was down and bleeding. Another onlooker ripped off his necktie and applied it as a tourniquet to the man's wound.

"Medics are here," Brunner said.

"I need a minute with this asshole," Cleaveland said, gesturing to the shooter. "You feel like you'll be able to join us at the capitol, Mr. Kaminsky?"

"Wouldn't miss it," Bobby said. "By the way, I've seen that SUV before, Detective. Twice for sure, maybe three times."

"Tell me about it later," Cleaveland said. "Meanwhile, get bandaged up and let's finish what we started."

· · ·

A paramedic cleaned the second gunshot wound Bobby had acquired since he'd started this adventure. Cleaveland got in the shooter's face. Micah leaned against the police cruisers, scribbling frantically in his notebook. Bobby had written scenes like this before, but he'd never been an active participant in one. Lindy was going to be pissed—again. He was getting a little long in the tooth for all this hands-on research.

Paramedics pronounced the driver of the black SUV dead at the scene.

"Did you get anything?" Bobby asked Detective Cleaveland.

"Oh yeah," Cleaveland said. "I got in his grill and said, 'I'm going to say two words to you, asshole. First word: Ianucci.' Asshole shook his head. 'Second word: Cavanaugh.' He looked like one of those Beatles bobble-heads singing 'yeah, yeah, yeah.'"

"Is Ianucci insulated here?" Bobby asked.

Detective Cleaveland pondered the question.

"Don't quote me on this, but I have a feeling Mr. Cavanaugh will happily roll on his boss in exchange for softening his own landing," he said. "Either way, it's a pretty good bet the senator's career in politics is over. The charges alone will have his money people running for cover."

Bobby, Micah, and the detectives made their way to the Pennsylvania State capitol building on North Third Street.

Chapter 20

Ed Ianucci was in a closed-door meeting with some funders for his gubernatorial campaign. Detective Cleaveland showed Ianucci's executive assistant his badge. Using his most imposing voice and looking exactly like a defensive tackle for the Mountaineers, he said, "Tell the senator this is a police matter of utmost urgency."

"You know, sir," she said, projecting the self-importance she was accustomed to seeing from her boss, "this building is, in legal terms, not in Harrisburg. It's the Commonwealth of Pennsylvania. I don't believe the Harrisburg Police Bureau has jurisdiction here."

Brunner's eyes bored into the young woman's soul. He punched a number into his phone while Cleaveland explained the penalties associated with Pennsylvania's obstruction of justice statute.

"Mr. Pepper," he said. "This is Detective Eric Brunner with the Harrisburg Police Bureau. Would you please dispatch a small contingent of Pennsylvania State Police to Senator Eduard Ianucci's office?" Ianucci's assistant turned and entered the senator's office. Brunner shrugged and showed the guys he'd been talking to himself.

Six suits exited the senator's office, followed by the officious assistant. Tommy Cavanaugh followed her, followed by the senator himself. He paused when he saw Micah and Bobby.

"Mr. Previn," Ianucci said. "I didn't expect to see you here. I saw the news."

"Save it, Senator," Micah said.

"Apparently your goons decided to commit felonious assault on the wrong person," Bobby said.

"I see you're still with us, Mr. Kaminski," Ianucci said. "That's unfortunate."

"Yeah, no thanks to you, Senator Asshole," Bobby said. Ianucci's eyes darkened.

"Do we do this out here, Senator? Or would you prefer the privacy of your office?" Cleaveland asked.

"Come in," he said. He turned to his assistant. "Get Bradley Wheeler over here. NOW!"

Ianucci closed the door and scanned his eyes from Cleaveland to Brunner to Bobby and then to Micah's battered face.

"Senator," Detective Cleaveland said. "We need to talk about Evelyn Marchesano."

Ianucci glanced between them.

"Who? Oh yes. Marchesano." Ianucci was terrible

at feigning recollection. "Of course. Garrett Bensen murdered Miss Marchesano in her home during his killing spree here in Harrisburg. It's a shame a weak judge threw out that portion of our case against him. I heard she was a lovely woman."

"It was Mrs. Marchesano," said Brunner. "She was married, Senator."

"Of course. Mrs. Marchesano," Ianucci said. "What about her?"

They were playing a game of bad cop/bad cop in the senator's office. Cleaveland was up to bat next.

"How long did you and Mrs. Marchesano carry on an affair before she demanded more? And when did you decide to murder her and let Cletus Tisdale clean up your mess?"

Ianucci gawked at Cleaveland. "Who? What? Who are you?"

Cleaveland held his gold shield close in front of Ed Ianucci's face.

"I'm Harrisburg Police Bureau Detective Earnest Cleaveland, and I asked you how long you had been fucking Evelyn Marchesano before you murdered her and hired a corrupt cop to cover it up?"

Ianucci was frozen. "I didn't—"

"Two other HPB detectives are debriefing Mr. Cavanaugh right now," Bobby said. "I'm sure he's sharing an interesting perspective of what occurred during your reign of terror in Dauphin County."

"Anything he says—" Ianucci started.

"Will be used against *you* in a court of law," said Cleaveland. "There's no statute of limitations on murder. But of course, you know that—being a lawyer and a former district attorney."

"And then," Bobby said, "there's the murder of Paul Winkler."

"I don't know who that is," said Ianucci. He paced behind his desk. "I won't be talked to like this. I'm a state senator. You will treat me with the respect and deference appropriate to the office."

He turned to Micah.

"Mr. Previn," he said, "I'm glad you're here. I'm glad someone from the press is here to witness and document this shameless attempt to slander my reputation and damage my campaign."

"Cletus Tisdale," Micah began. "The filthy cop you hired to do your dirty work? He kept a file of every job he ever did for you and Tommy Cavanaugh. Sergeant Tisdale left meticulous notes. Names, dates, photographs, even recorded testimony in his own voice. He detailed no less than eighteen crimes he and his crooked partners committed at the behest of you and Mr. Cavanaugh between 1988 and 1992—until Garrett Bensen put a stop to it in that alley off Peffer and North Third Street."

Bobby held up the files and recited the names. "Showalter, Callahan, Winkler, Marchesano, Bensen—"

"Bensen?" he shouted. "Bensen? Bensen confessed to—"

"Not Garrett Bensen," Micah said. "Kathy Cobb-Bensen, his wife, and their unborn child. You failed to ever prosecute anyone for her rape and murder on the streets of Harrisburg. That's how you gained the fealty and servitude of two corrupt cops and a convicted felon. You swept those cases out of your office and, in so doing, created your own personal hit squad."

"And then there are the crimes committed in the past several weeks. Attempted murder, at least three different times," Bobby said. "You and your boy, Tommy, have been very busy criminals."

"This is all Tommy Cavanaugh's doing," Ianucci said. "I knew nothing about any of it. If I had, I would have stopped it. I hope he's prosecuted—to the fullest extent of the law. I'll testify!"

They laughed.

"And this piece of fecal matter thought he was going to be governor, much less president of the United States," Bobby said.

"Cavanaugh's rolling on you right now, and here you are trying to roll on him. There really is no honor among thieves or murderers," Cleaveland said. "Mr. Previn, have you got all this straight for tomorrow's edition?"

Ianucci collapsed into his chair. His assistant barged in with the news that the senator's personal attorney, Bradley Wheeler, was in court and would call later.

"That's fine, have him meet his client at HPB Headquarters." Cleaveland said, then turned back to the senator. "Eduard Antonio Ianucci, you are under arrest for the murder of Evelyn Marchesano. You have the right to remain silent . . ."

Cleaveland completed Mirandizing and handcuffing Ianucci. They walked the senator out of his office and past his dumbstruck staff, minus Tommy Cavanaugh, who'd already been taken into custody. They marched down the marble steps of the capitol building. A horde of media, complete with microphones, recorders, lights, and cameras were waiting, compliments of Micah Previn, a satisfied smile on his bruised and battered face.

Chapter 21

Bobby looked forward to the drive to Waynesburg. He wanted to personally share the news with Garrett and with Jim Warren. For the moment though, Micah, Weldon Pepper, Earnest Cleaveland, and Bobby Kaminski shared a table at the Firehouse restaurant, enjoyed a lavish lunch on Weldon's American Express card, and reveled in the moment.

None of them were under any illusion that prosecuting Ed Ianucci for the murder of Evelyn Marchesano would be easy. The Charlotte files were iffy in terms of admissibility, and all who could directly point a finger at the senator with authority, except Tommy Cavanaugh, were dead. That said, the Amish gang who roughed up Micah, the shooter who twice attempted to murder Bobby Kaminski, and Fouser—if he could be persuaded to act in his own interest—could easily put the ambitious prosecutor away for decades. He might even spend time at Waynesburg, maybe even on Jim Warren's death row. But that was a too-good-to-be-true scenario.

Bobby spent his trip from Harrisburg to Waynesburg on the phone. He checked in with Jim Warren to let him know he had good news for Garrett. The warden chuckled when Bobby told him how things had played out with Ianucci.

"I guess I get to keep my job a little while longer."

His calls to Farmboy, Fatboy, and Cowboy were all hoots and hollers, like a bunch of teenagers celebrating a conquest.

Densmore heard from Al McCarthy directly: the motion had been granted and Prettyboy was out from under Ianucci's death sentence. Another glad tiding Bobby could share with his old roommate.

Fatboy wanted to know when they all could get together.

"Soon as we get word on clemency or a pardon, we'll set something up," Bobby said. "We need to plan a celebration."

"Oh, please, please leave that to me," Fatboy said. "I've got a couple of scenarios that will help introduce our Prettyboy back into the world."

Bobby wondered what shenanigans could be on Allebaugh's mind.

"I was actually thinking about right when he first gets released," Bobby said.

"Sounds like Farmboy has the rights to Garrett's first taste of freedom," Fatboy said. "The drug trial is a good way to set the table for his reentry."

"Yep," Bobby said. "A long-time-coming win for the kid."

Johnny Lee was ready. He was as jacked as Bobby ever remembered, which was saying something.

"We keep a small place in Durham we stay at during football and basketball season. I'll set him up there while he's doing the trial. Help him find some work, keep him busy when he's not . . . trialing drugs or whatever all that means."

"Just remember," Bobby cautioned. "If it happens—when it happens—he'll be getting out after twenty-three years on death row, Farmboy. That's a huge chunk of his life. And the world has changed a lot since 1994."

They hadn't yet considered any restrictions the governor might place on Garrett's release. Would he still have to serve time? Would he be required to remain in the jurisdiction of the court? Would he be on any kind of probation? If so, how long? Would there be terms attached to any pardon? These were questions for Weldon Pepper and Al McCarthy. In the short haul, though, it seemed to Bobby like Johnny and Shelby were ready to adopt Prettyboy.

It was six When Bobby pulled into the parking lot at SCI-Greene. The sun sat low in the west and a few high clouds punctuated the otherwise blue Pennsylvania sky. There were only a couple cars in the lot. A guard who looked to Bobby like he'd just entered puberty approached.

"Excuse me, sir. Are you Mr. Kaminsky?" he asked.

"I sure am, Mr. . . . Patton," Bobby said, noting the guard's name badge.

"Warden Warren asked me to escort you."

"Escort away, young fella," he said.

Patton mumbled something into a walkie talkie.

They went through six locked gates, crossed a short hallway Bobby had not traveled previously, and turned a corner. Jim Warren stood there, smiling. Standing alongside him was Garrett Bensen, unshackled, grinning from ear to ear. They walked toward each other slowly, falling into a long, peaceful hug that left both of them in tears. The warden smiled.

"Bobby fucking K. from Sheepshead fucking Bay," Garrett said.

"We can talk in the office," said the warden. "Then I'll leave you two lovebirds alone for a while."

Bobby regaled Jim and Garrett with his three-day/two-night odyssey in the capital city of Pennsylvania.

Garrett asked about Micah Previn. Warren wanted to know what Bobby thought of Weldon Pepper. He told them the real stars of the show were Charlotte Tisdale and Detective Earnest Cleaveland. Garrett was overwhelmed. After all that time, there was a witness to what happened in that alley off Peffer Street. He'd thought there was but was never sure of it.

"Fact is," Bobby said, "the way the detective described it to his chain of command, and then to Weldon Pepper—who, by the way, deserves at least an honorable mention in all that's happened—and the way Pepper retold it to me, despite what we know from your own account of things, there is reason to believe you might have acted in self-defense. Detective Cleaveland described you as 'one badass dude.'"

"So," Jim Warren said. "What happens next?"

"Am I really getting out of here?" Garrett asked, incredulous.

"Right now, that's in the hands of the governor," Bobby said. "Cowboy, that's Bill Densmore," he explained for Warren's sake, "has a friend who sits on the Pennsylvania Supreme Court."

"I have a scorecard over there on my desk," Warren said. "Cowboy, Fatboy, Farmboy, Cityboy and . . ." He shook his head. "Prettyboy, right?"

"Right," Bobby said. Back to Garrett. "Your sentence will likely be commuted. If that happens, Weldon Pepper says there's a chance you'll be released based on time served."

Bobby explained the possibility of the drug trial.

"How does that work?" Garrett asked.

"You get to be a guinea pig for some pharmaceutical operation while you hang out around Duke's medical center. And you know," he continued, "I have it on pretty good authority that there are coeds in the vicinity of Duke University." That got an eye roll from the warden and a classic Prettyboy smile from Garrett.

Jim Warren told them to take all the time they

needed. He was heading home to open a bottle of thirty-year-old Scotch.

"I'd invite you over, but he's still a prisoner," he said, nodding at Garrett. "For now, anyway."

"What's your experience in things like this?" Bobby asked him.

The warden laughed. "Things like this? Gentlemen," he said, "I have never experienced anything like this. I'll check in with Weldon Pepper tomorrow, and we'll go from there."

Garrett shook the warden's hand. Warren looked at his hand.

"That's another thing I don't have much experience with," Warren said. "Guys on the row don't shake hands with the warden of the penitentiary. See you tomorrow, Garrett. We'll figure out where you get to live now that you're officially off the row."

"Off the row," Garrett repeated. He swallowed. "Off death row."

The one-time roommates spent another hour of Garrett asking, and Bobby attempting to answer a whole range of questions. He wanted to know how Bobby's book was going to play out. Garrett wondered whether he should ask to stay in his room on the row or move into the general prison population. He asked about Monika Densmore, Charlotte Tisdale, Allebaugh's partner, Johnny's family, Lindy, and Bobby's adult daughters. It occurred to both of them that they'd never taken even a moment to talk about any of that until now.

"You know, Prettyboy," Bobby said. "This might be a good time to reach out to Ingrid."

Tears welled up in Garrett's eyes. "Yeah, I thought about that. I wouldn't even know what to say to her."

"I think she'd be psyched to hear from her big brother," Bobby said.

Garrett nodded. "Let's see how things go," he said.

It occurred to Bobby that the last time the five of them had been together in one place was the day before Bobby left Darmstadt for Samsun, Turkey. That was over thirty-two years ago, in 1984. When would they all be together next? And under what circumstances might that be?

Chapter 22

Bobby stopped by SCI-Greene before heading to PIT for his flight home. Garrett stayed where he was, pending word from the governor's office. Weldon Pepper told Jim Warren to expect news within a month, two at the most.

"They're going to do extensive research," Warren said. "First, they'll review gubernatorial pardons in Pennsylvania over the last hundred years or so, for precedent. The governor's reelection campaign will contract for research to determine the substance of a message platform aimed at voters. Probably both qualitative and quantitative stuff, like a poll of at least four hundred voters, and a half-dozen focus groups," he said. "I know a bit about how political campaigns work. Nothing happens without testing it first."

All this was beyond any of their control.

After Garrett went back to his cell, Bobby broke the news to Jim Warren about Dave Fouser having been on Ed Ianucci's payroll. At first, he was crushed, but when Bobby told the warden how Fouser copped to everything he did, and when he considered what Fouser had given up so nothing would splatter on the warden, he felt a little better about the deal Harrisburg police would offer him to testify against Ianucci and Cavanaugh.

"I couldn't figure out for the life of me why a guy like Garrett Bensen was on death row in the first place," Warren said. "He and I have been sharing space for a long time. He is just not the type. But you never know people."

"Then there's your guy, Fouser," Bobby said. Jim Warren shook his head.

"He was solid, the most dependable CO I had on the row," he said. "I know these officers don't get paid nearly enough for the work they do. I know about his daughter's health. But if someone asked me who the last guy would be to take bribes, I would have said Dave Fouser."

"Don't spend a lot of time trying to find answers," Bobby said. "People are people. We're all of us just human. Even the best of us do some stupid shit."

They said their goodbyes. Bobby promised to be back when the gates at SCI-Greene opened and Garrett Bensen walked out.

• • •

Bobby ruminated over what Warren said about never really knowing people. When the public really got wind of who and what Senator Ianucci was, their judgment would be swift and certain. It might be more complicated in court, but Ianucci would never be a public figure again.

As far as the Filthy Five were concerned, any comparisons between who they were when they were young and who they became would be wasted effort. Johnny Lee was the only one who hadn't changed much. He'd been a farm boy when he enlisted and he was a farmer now. As for the rest of them, who possibly could have imagined or foreseen one would be a solid citizen lawyer, another would be a gay real estate executive, or that Bobby would become a best-selling author? Then he turned his thoughts to Garrett Bensen.

He couldn't even begin to imagine any of what that kid had gone through.

• • •

Forty-one days after he'd returned home from Waynesburg, Bobby got a call from Weldon Pepper.

"Tomorrow morning, Governor Hill will sign a declaration of clemency for Garrett Bensen, releasing him from the custody of the Commonwealth of Pennsylvania, without restriction," he said. "He's served more than sufficient time for the crimes he committed. He can live wherever he wants. He's free to travel. He can get a passport. He can vote. Hell, in some states, not here, but in some, he can even own a firearm. He has paid his debt. God bless America, right?"

Bobby let the warm wave wash over him. His book would have a most satisfying ending. *God bless the governor of Pennsylvania*, Bobby thought.

"When can he leave?" Bobby asked.

"As soon as the document hits the warden's inbox," Weldon said. "With processing and a physical, that will be sometime day after tomorrow. What's the plan?"

"Sending him to that clinical trial at Duke. One of our old crew is an alum. He believes he can get Garrett into the trial."

"Great first step," Weldon said. "You know, Bob, I'm not sure I ever thanked you. I know the governor's re-election wasn't the reason you did what you did, but the net effect is, he's going to run unopposed next month."

"You're more than welcome, Weldon. Consider it a collateral benefit. Please extend my gratitude to him for the clemency," he said. "There are so many ways this could have all gone to hell in a handbag. I'm glad it worked out the way it did."

"Keep in touch," Weldon said. "You and Mrs. Bobby K. from Sheepshead Bay need to be on the lookout for an invitation to the inauguration."

"Wow! Harrisburg in January," Bobby said. "Can't wait."

• • •

The four all showed up for Garrett's release. Bobby flew in from Florida, Johnny drove from North Carolina, and Bill and CW arrived via Densmore's younger brother's corporate jet. The band was almost back together for the first time in over thirty-two years.

Allebaugh decreed the event be handled in appropriately dramatic fashion. Through an introduction from Bobby, Fatboy instructed Jim Warren to buy Garrett a pair of new black slacks, a pair of black loafers, a pale blue dress shirt, black socks, and new underwear, all on Cowboy's credit card. They were waiting outside the gate, similarly attired, head to toe—except they all wore brand-new camelhair jackets, complete with embroidered crests.

The warden and Garrett walked out. As soon as he spotted them, Garrett laughed like a crazy person. He hugged Bobby, Densmore, and Johnny. When he approached Fatboy, a man he wouldn't have recognized under any circumstance, Allebaugh swept a jacket from behind his back and threw it over Garrett's shoulders as if Prettyboy had just won the Masters.

"You guys are absolutely friggin' nuts," Garrett said. He was laughing, but his tears were real.

Everyone thanked Jim Warren, who made Bobby promise to keep in touch. Bobby told the warden to expect a signed copy of the book as soon as it was published. Then they were on their way.

• • •

They drove up to Pittsburgh in a two-car caravan; Fatboy, Cowboy, and Prettyboy in an SUV Densmore had rented, followed by Bobby and Johnny in Farmboy's tricked out F-150. They had a great dinner at the Hofbrauhaus. Everyone around them wondered about the jackets. When their server finally asked about them, Allebaugh was ready.

"You, young lady," he said, "are witness to a slice of genuine American history. We at this table are the sole surviving members of a team of reprobates who helped save our nation from the last vestiges of the Cold War. And this man, right here"—he pointed at Prettyboy—"is our fearless leader, who we," whispering now, "just broke out of the prison at Waynesburg. Don't say anything to anyone!" He made the "zip your lips" gesture.

She looked at the five of them for a moment with world-weary eyes. They all looked back at her, expectantly.

"Cool," she deadpanned. "Nice jackets. You dudes ready to order?"

. . .

Johnny and Garrett learned there would be a two-month wait for the next testing cycle in the Duke trial. Since Garrett had no home to return to, the Filthy Five's de facto social director, C. W. Allebaugh, eased their friend back into American society. He scheduled Prettyboy for consecutive weeklong visits with each of them, leaving Johnny's farm and family for last.

Reorientation for someone who's been out of the American swirl for decades can be daunting. Except for his stints in basic training in San Antonio and technical training in Biloxi, Garrett Bensen had never been further west than Minnesota. After his release, he spent time in southwest Florida with Bobby and Lindy, in Santa Fe with Bill and Monika Densmore, and in San Francisco with C. W. Allebaugh and Mike Tomczak.

During that "national tour"—which Allebaugh memorialized on limited edition T-shirts for each of them: black with gold lettering, and which looked fashionably cool under camelhair jackets—Garrett got acquainted with the country he'd served in the 1980s and discovered how much he didn't know about life in the new millennium.

It didn't take him long, but he had to relearn to drive. New generation household appliances, such as advanced microwave ovens and food processors, amazed him. Bobby taught him how to operate a smart phone and a MacBook Pro, how to navigate the internet, and all the joys and frustrations of satellite television. Allebaugh helped him with the supermarkets and other big box retailers. The list was endless. The world, especially in America, and especially in the digital age, changes a great deal in nearly a quarter-century.

The one thing Garrett didn't need to relearn was how to interact with women.

As his physical condition began to improve, he discovered Whole Foods Market. He couldn't get his head around some of the prices. The products were equally mysterious. But it was there, in Raleigh, where he met a divorcée in her early forties. She was cheese shopping; he was coming to terms with the reality of $18/pound Havarti. She bought him a cup of organic coffee. Prettyboy was still Prettyboy.

Her name was Jill. His name should have been Jack.

• • •

The ninety-day clinical trial in Durham and the eight-week drug regimen did the trick. Five short months after he began treatment, Garrett Bensen was declared free of the viral infection that had inflamed his liver and attacked healthy cells in his body. Johnny and Shelby made sure all his basic needs were met while he participated in the trial. Garrett found a job in Raleigh working in the kitchen of a nonprofit shelter for homeless veterans.

After over twenty years on death row, Garrett Bensen was free, healthy, and ready to face whatever the future had in store for him.

Chapter 23

Six months after the clinical trial ended, Garrett was at JDL Dairies, learning the process of helping get the most out of a large herd of Holstein dairy cows. Bobby checked in and was told by Farmboy, "The kid's a natural."

"Glad to hear it," Bobby said.

"The girls love him, Bobby," he said. "I think ol' Prettyboy has a future in milk."

"You guys like having him around?"

"You bet!" Farmboy said. He'd just promoted Garrett to a full-time second to the farm foreman. "He's gonna help us expand our operation and move into new markets."

One day, out of the blue, Garrett asked for a few days off to go to Pittsburgh. He wanted to visit Kathy.

"I need to see her," he said. "I hope you guys don't mind, but I want to do this by myself." Johnny called Bobby for counsel.

"He hasn't really been out of our sight, you know,"

Johnny said. "You think he's ready to go back there? Relive all that stuff?"

Bobby had no hesitation.

"He lived in a cage for a long time," he said. "He's been a Boy Scout since he got out. Hell, he's the same kid we knew way back in the day. He can do this."

• • •

Garrett made the trip in a new Kia Sorrento, for which Johnny had cosigned. On his way back, Bobby called.

"There's a reason for this call, besides checking in on you." Bobby said. "First, tell me about the trip."

He told Cityboy that in 1989, after the coroner released her body, Kathy's parents brought her home to Pittsburgh. They were angry but quickly forgave Garrett. He'd done what he'd done and was in prison, sentenced to die. The Colonel visited him once and told him where Kathy was at rest—Calvary Cemetery in Pittsburgh.

"Just before I started on the drug trial," Garrett told Bobby. "I called the Cobbs. They were listed in the Pittsburgh phone directory. The conversation was uncomfortable but cordial. The colonel is eighty-one now and has arthritis. Kathy's mom is seventy-eight and dealing with diabetes. They're retired and living in a neighborhood near the heart of the city. I told them as much as I could about my release from prison. They were happy for me, but like me, they miss their daughter every day."

"I was somewhere in West Virginia," Garrett said. "I called Colonel and Mrs. Cobb to tell them I was coming to see Kathy. I told them I was on my way and asked if they'd like to join me. They declined but let me know where she was and asked me to send her their love.

"After a good night's sleep," he said, "I got breakfast and headed to the cemetery. I wanted to get on the road back home as soon as I finished my visit."

"You must have really struggled with all this," Bobby said.

"I was a mess, Bobby," he said. "I stopped at the cemetery office and got a little map with directions to where she was. It killed me. I couldn't see her, touch her, or hold her. When I found her, I was stunned. Her parents had bought a double plot and a double headstone. Apparently, they'd made my arrangements along with hers. They must have expected I'd be executed."

"I wish I remembered the Cobbs better," Bobby said. "These are special people."

"They are. And they raised a really special girl," Garrett said. "The inscription read *Katherine Anastasia Cobb-Bensen*—I had to smile at that; she was hot and cold about her middle name—*Beloved daughter, wife, mother, and teacher.*

"I put a bouquet of flowers against the tombstone. Then I spoke to her."

"You don't have to tell me all this if you don't want to," Bobby said.

"I do. I want to. I said, 'Kathy, honey. I am so sorry. I'm sorry I couldn't protect you. I'm sorry I ever took you to Harrisburg. I'm sorry we never got to know our baby. I'm sorry for what those miserable bastards did to you. I'm sorry for the awful things I did because of what they did to you. I love you, even today. I'll always love you, no matter what.'

"I told her, 'Kat'—that's what I used to call her, Kat—'I've lived a long, long time alone, mostly waiting to die. My friends from Germany, I know you'd remember at least a couple of them, well, they managed to help me get out of prison and get my health back; and, now that I'm, I guess, middle-aged, to have something resembling a life.'"

Bobby took a pull on a bottle of water. He was pretty sure Garrett was holding things together by a thread. He worried about all this coming out while Garrett was dodging big rigs on some interstate highway.

"I had to let her know why I was there," Garrett said. "I told her I came to see her because someone has come into my life, a really sweet woman. 'She's not replacing you,' I said. 'Nobody can ever replace you. Her name is Jill. We're moving in together. Maybe sometime down the road . . .'"

"She knows everything there is to know about me and you, and she still wants to be with me. It's not fair, I know that Kat, but I'm . . . I'm just so tired of being alone . . .

He paused.

"After that, I stood there. I don't know for how long. And finally, finally, after all those years, I just cried it all out. When I finished, I looked at the stone, the place reserved, I suppose, for me," he said.

"I told her, 'Looks like your mom and the Colonel saved a place for me here. I'm grateful they no longer blame me for what happened. I still blame myself. That's something I'll live with until my time comes to be with you again. I love you, Kathy Anastasia. I miss you every day. I miss our baby. I miss our life. I'll come see you again, honey. I promise.'"

Bobby waited while Garrett collected himself.

"I stood there with my hand on the stone. Then I got back on the road to Durham."

"I don't know what to say," Bobby said.

"I know," he said. Neither spoke.

"Listen, Prettyboy, I really appreciate you sharing all this with me, but I called because I have some news for you," Bobby said. "Have you heard from any of the other guys yet today?"

"Not today," he said. "Cowboy's been keeping me updated with news from Al McCarthy and his friend on the Supreme Court. He mentioned Ianucci's up-coming trial. They let him out on bail, but he has to check in every day and wear some kind of ankle thing.

"Ankle monitor," Bobby said. "If he wasn't who he was, he'd never have seen the light of day."

"That's what Densmore said. Seemed like they moved a lot faster when it was me on trial. Confessing really wasn't the smartest thing I ever did."

No, it wasn't, Bobby thought, choosing not to pile on.

"Cowboy says Ianucci's definitely going to be convicted for the poisoning, the car antics, and Micah's beating. Said they were legal slam-dunks."

Everything else had depended on whether the judge would allow Charlotte Tisdale's files into evidence. It could go either way. Without Tisdale or either of the others alive to testify, the files might constitute unsubstantiated hearsay evidence and could deny Ianucci his constitutional right to confront his accuser. But because several of the relevant files contained actual audiotapes in Tisdale's own voice, and because they were brought to light by Tisdale's widow, the judge might admit those without establishing firm grounds for overturn on appeal.

"Where are you right now?" Bobby asked.

Garrett hesitated. "I'm actually not sure. I drove up by way of West Virginia . . . , so I decided to drive back on I-81, down through the Shenandoah Valley in Virginia. I picked it up just west of Harrisburg . . . Okay . . . it seems like I just crossed into Maryland."

Bobby smiled. "You're wearing your seatbelt, right?"

Garrett laughed. "Uh, yeah. They've really gotten stricter about these belts since the last time I drove."

"I have news, and better news," Bobby said. "I got a call earlier from Weldon. Ed Ianucci killed himself this morning, right after the trial judge ruled that Charlotte Tisdale's files would be admitted into evidence."

Garrett didn't respond.

"You there, Prettyboy?" Bobby asked. "Did you hear . . ."

This was what they hoped would happen. Not Ianucci killing himself, but that the evidence would be admitted. And Ianucci would cut some kind of deal before the jury could even hear it in order to avoid the death penalty. None of them ever thought a narcissistic, sociopathic bastard like him might take his own life.

"I just got off the phone with Al McCarthy," Bobby said. "With Ianucci dead and Cavanaugh in prison, he couldn't see any need for a trial."

No trial. Garrett Bensen's long ordeal truly, officially, finally was now over.

"You there, Garrett?" Bobby asked. "Did I lose you?"

"No, Cityboy," Garrett said. "You didn't lose me. I'm right here."

"It's over, Prettyboy," Bobby said. "It's all over."

"What they say is true. Man plans, God laughs," Garrett said. "Life really depends on random shit falling into place."

"Random shit?" Bobby asked. "What kind of random shit?"

"If the Filthy Five hadn't intervened, if Micah Previn didn't write about a possible witness, if Detective Cleaveland didn't read the newspaper, if Weldon Pepper didn't get involved. Even Fouser. If he didn't confess to you and then finally give it all up in that deposition. And Charlotte—if you don't find her, and if she doesn't didn't find that box of files. . .. Everything had to happen so I could get released and get well. Shit, I could have been dead several different ways by now."

He was right, of course, Bobby thought. *A bunch of random factors came together and made all the difference in the world.*

"Hell," Garrett continued. "If you hadn't seen that news story in *USA Today* and started making phone calls . . . Shit, Bobby, we were just kids in the service, doing our jobs, having fun, growing up. So much random stuff, good stuff, had to happen after so much bad stuff had already happened."

"Every bit was worth it," Bobby said. "Every damn bit."

Garrett made it back to Blakesville, North Carolina, where he met Jill, the Lee family, and the JDL organization. He brought a blank page on which he could write his own plan, whatever it may be, for the rest of his life.

• • •

The next day, *USA Today* had a freestanding news item on page five, under the headline, "Disgraced Pennsylvania Gubernatorial Candidate Takes Own Life."

Former Pennsylvania State Senator
and gubernatorial candidate Eduard

Ianucci, who was facing a variety of charges stemming from the 1993 trial and conviction of confessed triple murderer Garrett Bensen, was found inside his car in the garage of his suburban Harrisburg home, dead of asphyxiation due to carbon monoxide poisoning. He was 54 years old.

Ianucci, a former Dauphin County (PA) district attorney, rose to prominence following the conviction of Garrett Bensen, who confessed to murdering Harrisburg Police Bureau Sergeant Cletus Tisdale, former HPB officer Arthur Sheffield, and Joseph DiStefano, a career criminal, in 1991.

Bensen was scheduled to die by lethal injection in September of last year when new evidence came to light, along with eyewitness testimony, which resulted in Bensen having his death sentence commuted by Governor Tom Hill.

A spokesman for Gov. Hill said a ruling allowing highly damaging evidence into the upcoming trial of the senator's involvement in a decades-long criminal conspiracy, including crimes committed at his direction by Tisdale, Sheffield, and DiStefano, was likely the impetus for the suicide.

According to a spokesman for trial judge, Susan Morgenstern, "The information contained in the Tisdale files was confirmed by Sen. Ianucci's former aide, Thomas Cavanaugh, as part of his own plea arrangement with the State."

"Ianucci was already facing up to 21 years in prison for his part in ordering the attempted murders of Garrett Bensen and author Robert Kaminski, a friend of Bensen's, and for criminal facilitation by ordering a violent and vicious assault on Harrisburg Patriot-News reporter Micah Previn in the weeks leading up to Bensen's pardon," said Weldon Pepper, chief of staff to Governor Hill.

"The ruling allowing taped and written notes kept by Cletus Tisdale, and corroborated by Tom Cavanaugh, into Ianucci's trial appeared to be the final blow."

• • •

Bobby walked through the French patio doors of his and Lindy's Gulf-front condo. She was there, reading that day's papers. She closed them and patted the cushion of the rattan loveseat next to where she was sitting.

"Looks like a good ending," she said. "Is Garrett okay?"

Bobby smiled and plopped down next to her. "As was the case yesterday, Garrett is just fine and dandy."

He picked up the glass of Chardonnay. "And so, my love, are the clowns and thieves in New York. Or they will be when I send them the final chapter."

They watched the sun slowly descend into the Gulf of Mexico as they did most evenings, holding hands and sipping wine. Bobby recalled that day in the United Airlines lounge, the back and forth with his agent Doug Soskin, and the sense of dread he'd felt at the time. He had worried the reservoir of words might finally have run dry.

"What'cha thinkin', Bobby K. from Sheepshead Bay?" Lindy asked, flashing that smile that still melted his heart.

"Something Garrett said when we talked yesterday," he said. "About random factors all having to come together so something good could happen." He recounted all that had to happen so Garrett Bensen could gain his freedom and Bobby could deliver his book to a skeptical publisher.

"You know me," Lindy said, refilling both their wine glasses. "I never for a second doubted you'd knock it out of the park for Garrett."

It had been eighteen months since Garrett's sentence was commuted. The wheels of justice had moved agonizingly slowly but still arrived at their appropriate destination. Bobby couldn't muster any sympathy for the disgraced senator; he was just happy that Garrett wouldn't have to deal with the three-ring circus of a trial.

It would still be several months before *The Filthy Five: A Story of Friendship, Murder, and Redemption* would hit bookstore shelves. It was time for Bobby to consider what was next.

For now, as far as Cityboy Bobby Kaminsky was concerned, the Filthy Five were once again intact, and he had a most satisfying finish to his book.

End

Acknowledgments

The author would like to thank so, so many people who have knowingly or otherwise supported this effort, including but not limited to the Katz, Medlar, Foster, Diehn, and Van Oss families; friends and colleagues in both western North Carolina and central Florida; professors and fellow students from Valencia College, Rollins College, and Western Carolina University; and even a few OLD friends from long ago in Brooklyn, New York, and the United States air force. Some may recognize pieces and aspects of themselves on these pages, while others may wonder why they've been forgotten. They haven't.

Thanks to Robert Kenney of Thoughtful Editing, Victoria Griffin, and Anna Krusinski from Blue Pen. Thanks to Ron Rash, Pam Duncan, Bob Morris, Ilyse Kusnetz, and Steven Cooper for their wisdom, advice, counsel, and encouragement through the years.

Special thanks always to Lynn, for putting up with all the hours of closed doors and both quiet keystrokes and noisy grumbling emanating from the back room.

About the Author

Bruce F. Katz—Bud to his friends—is author of the business biography, *When Your Name Is On the Door*, along with novels, *The History Lesson* (YA), and *The Family Jewels*. He grew up in Brooklyn, New York and served four years in the US Air Force. He was graduated Magna Cum Laude from Western Carolina University with a BA in English. A retired strategic communication, mass media, advertising, and public relations executive, he lives with his wife, Lynn, a former defense and aerospace industry executive, in Highlands, North Carolina.